D0407585

THE QUIET HERO

THE UNTOLD MEDAL OF HONOR STORY OF
GEORGE E. WAHLEN
AT THE
BATTLE FOR IWO JIMA

BY GARY W. TOYN

Copyright © 2006 By Gary W. Toyn

Published by
American Legacy Media
1544 W. 1620 N. STE 1
Clearfield, Utah 84015-8243
Visit us at www.americanlegacymedia.com

Illustration on page 139 courtesy Robert D. De Geus; Illustration on page 61 courtesy Richard E. Overton, from *God Isn't Here: A Young American's entry into World War II and his Participation in the Battle for Iwo Jima*, Copyright © 2004.

Cover design by Hillary Wallace
Pacific map on page 4-5 by William D. Wood
Author photo by Zachary Williams

ISBN 10: 0-9761547-1-4
ISBN 13: 978-0-9761547-1-6

Printed in Canada
Library of Congress Control Number: 2005926264
Cataloging-in-Publication Data - Provided by Quality Books

  Toyn, Gary W.
  The quiet hero : the untold medal of honor story of
  George E. Wahlen at the battle for Iwo Jima / by Gary W.
  Toyn ; foreword by Senator Robert J. "Bob" Dole ;
  introduction by Senator Orrin G. Hatch. -- 1st ed.
  p. cm.
  Includes bibliographical references and index.
  ISBN 0-9761547-1-4

  1. Wahlen, George E., 1924- 2. Iwo Jima, Battle of,
  Japan, 1945--Personal narratives, American. 3. United
  States. Marine Corps--Biography. 4. Medal of Honor--
  Biography. I. Title.
  D767.99.I9.T69 2005 940.54'2528'092
      QBI05-600004

Set in Baskerville and Copperplate

ACCLAIM FOR "THE QUIET HERO"

(*The Quiet Hero*) serves as a means of preserving the legacy of a genuine American hero, it is not just a biography; it stands as a tribute to a nation that willingly thrust its most accomplished and capable young people into harm's way."   — Senator Bob Dole

"The George Wahlen story is one of inspiration and motivation for all of us who came from humble beginnings, and made the best with what God has given us."
                                                                        — Senator Orrin Hatch

"The Battle for Iwo Jima was the only battle during World War II in which the Americans suffered more casualties than the enemy. Like many who served on Iwo Jima, George Wahlen endured more than his share of misery and death, and he has carried those excruciating memories silently over the past six decades. Fortunately the astonishing details of how he earned the Medal of Honor are at long last available for all to appreciate. *The Quiet Hero* offers an extraordinary peek into the making of one of our nation's most distinguished war heroes."
                —James Bradley, author of national best-sellers *Flags of Our Fathers* and *Flyboys*

"*The Quiet Hero* gives the reader a compelling daily account of the hells of combat on Iwo Jima, in 1945, one of the bloodiest battles in Marine Corps history."
                — Harlan Glenn, Author/Historian/Technical Advisor - Harlans-Heroes.com

Gary Toyn has effectively researched the life and heroic actions of Navy Corpsman George Wahlen, weaving the young man's personal history into a riveting and historically accurate account of his heroism at Iwo Jima. It is a rare glimpse of the qualities that are common in society, that yield heroes of legendary remembrance."
                — C. Douglas Sterner, Medal of Honor Authority, Founder of HomeofHeroes.com

"*The Quiet Hero* is one of those rare books that can transport you to this forsaken island, and give you a glimpse of how a few men experienced this historic battle. This book is long overdue, as every American should come to know why George Wahlen earned this country's highest honor for valor."   — Dean Keeley, Ph.D., Iwo Jima Veteran

"I've not seen many books that so graphically and authentically portray battle. Few war books are so well documented... The pictures complement the text most effectively, (and) is most authentic."
                — Don Norton, WWII Historian, Brigham Young University

"*The Quiet Hero* is a unique book about an uncommonly good man.   For anyone interested in learning more about the Battle for Iwo Jima, this book offers a different prospective and sheds new light on the relationship created between the corpsman and the Marine in combat."
                — Rudolph T. Mueller, Fox Co., 2/26, 5th Marine Div., Rifleman

"*The Quiet Hero* is an unforgettable story about the quintessential WWII hero. His story is inspiring and heart-wrenching, and comes at you with the intensity uncommon to most biographies."
                — Robert D. De Geus, Fox Co., 2/26, 5th Marine Div., Corpsman

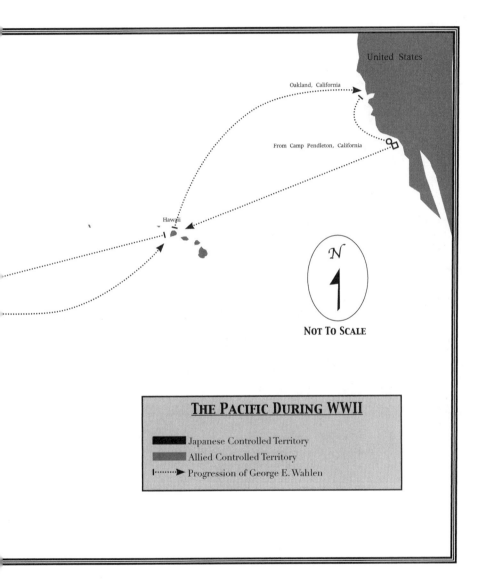

United States

Oakland, California

From Camp Pendleton, California

Hawaii

𝒩
↑
NOT TO SCALE

THE PACIFIC DURING WWII

Japanese Controlled Territory
Allied Controlled Territory
Progression of George E. Wahlen

George E. Wahlen, 1943

Contents

FOREWORD

SENATOR ROBERT J. DOLE

The character of a nation can well be determined by how it pays homage to its heroes. The Medal of Honor is this country's highest honor for valor in combat, and has been awarded to fewer than 3,500 recipients throughout our nation's long history.

From the moment this nation learned of the attack on Pearl Harbor, Americans began mobilizing in an unprecedented manner, as the very existence of the nation was at stake. The Second World War was not only the defining event of the 20th century; it defined a great generation of people who confronted some of history's greatest tyrants. Their fidelity to the cause never failed, although their resoluteness was often tested.

During this epic world war, the Medal of Honor was presented to 198 living recipients. Throughout the past sixty years, these honored veterans have dignified our country with a legacy of nobility and inspiration. But even war heroes are mortal, and they cannot avoid the unmerciful march through life. The inevitable reunion with their beloved comrades cannot long be averted.

Within these pages you will read about George E. Wahlen and his participation in the Battle for Iwo Jima, the most costly battle of World War II. As with any account of war, you can expect gruesome descriptions of unspeakable horror. But you will also gain a glimpse of how men, in a struggle for survival, endured a breadth of emotions ranging from devotion to despair, weariness to grief, and hostility to joy.

Mr. Wahlen was one of 27 men decorated with the Medal of Honor during the 36-day battle for this forsaken island that was critical to the success of the Pacific war. He was among many brave men about whose mettle Fleet Admiral Chester W. Nimitz commented: "Uncommon valor was a common virtue."

This book serves as a means of preserving the legacy of a genuine American hero, and the memories of a handful of his revered comrades. It is not just a biography; it stands as a tribute to a nation that willingly thrust its most accomplished and capable young people into harm's way, to exact justice upon the oppressors and liberate the oppressed. I hope you will draw inspiration from the many acts of courage and valor described herein. May our Creator bless this great nation, and the precious freedoms such heroes paid so dearly to preserve.

Introduction

By Senator Orrin G. Hatch

Six decades since the aftermath of World War II, we remember the sacrifices of more than 16 million of this country's brightest young people, who united to fight an enemy against whom we could not suffer defeat. Many historians agree that the aftermath of the Second World War brought about America's second revolution. Even today, we still experience the long-term effects from the aftermath of this conflict, both in world politics and in American culture. Most changes have been for the good, but undoubtedly the world has never been the same since.

So many years removed from these events, a generation is being raised without understanding the true cost of their comfortable lifestyles. Even those of us who remember living through the War may still fail to remember that the catalysts of these changes —changes which gave us our current social well-being and status in the world —were the men who fought, suffered, and died to win this epic conflict between good and evil.

To those whose lives were cut short, who sacrificed themselves to preserve our way of life, we owe a great debt of gratitude. To paraphrase John Maxwell Edmonds "They gave their tomorrows, so that we may have our todays." Amazingly, it took 59 years for this country to honor this "Greatest Generation" with a monument on the National Mall in Washington, DC. But for over 400,000 families, the memories of their fallen warriors have never faded.

As a scrawny 10-year-old boy in Pittsburgh, I remember dashing home one February afternoon in 1945 to find a man in uniform consoling my parents. My older brother Jess was a nose-gunner in a B-24 Liberator and the military officer was there to report that Jess's plane had been shot down over Austria. Indelibly etched in my mind is the scene of my mother sobbing at the news that Jess was presumed dead. I was physically ill at the news, and despite my thin, gangly frame, couldn't eat for days. The events of that day had a profound effect on me, and the emotions I experienced then are still fresh in my mind.

My respect for my fallen brother has grown over time, as I have learned even more of his bravery and valor during his shortened military career. I later learned that he had been shot down twice before his fatal flight, and both times was secreted back to safety by the brave civilians of the underground resistance. You see, Jess was not only my big brother, he was my hero. What I didn't know at that young age was that Jess represented a host of heroes that would ultimately contribute to victory of this war.

My brother, the men of his bomber crew, and all those who bravely fought the Axis forces, were heroic because they repeatedly placed their lives in danger to complete their missions. Likewise, the men and women of the underground resistance were heroic, as they worked together, risking their lives to save my brother, and countless other air crews who were shot down behind enemy lines. Heroism of this kind was common in wartime, as millions of soldiers, sailors, airmen, Marines and Coast Guardsmen, along with our allies, risked their lives to battle the Axis powers.

Another, more uncommon, class of hero came in the form of individuals who single-handedly saved the lives of others, or who disregarded their own safety for the benefit of others. This type of hero is recognized for valor and intrepidity, and in rare cases is decorated with an official medal. In America, the highest medal for valor in combat is the Medal of Honor. Fewer than 500 men received this medal during World War II and less than half of those men survived to tell their heroic story.

These true American heroes were recognized for their bravery and returned home to a hero's welcome, but in the decades since World War II, have gone on to live quiet, productive lives. Their stories provide inspiration to future generations, and give further evidence that heroism never dies.

Throughout the years, a small number of these Medal of Honor recipients have published their war-time stories, and left a legacy for future generations. Unfortunately, many more heroes have passed on with little or none of their story made available. As this "Greatest Generation" matures, we are losing an estimated 1,000 World War II veterans each day, and unfortunately, many of these inspirational stories are being lost forever.

Among the many stories that should be told, is that of George E. Wahlen. George was a Navy corpsman who volunteered to serve with a Marine infantry unit in 1944. After an intense year of training, his Marine unit boarded one of the hundreds of ships destined for the unknown island of Iwo Jima.

The Battle for Iwo Jima was one of the most critical battles of World War II. It was necessary for the U.S. to control this island's airstrips, so they could bomb Japan with the same frequency and intensity that ultimately lead to Germany's capitulation.

Before the battle, U.S. commanders knew of the perilous struggle ahead. One military commander stated that "Iwo Jima was the most heavily fortified and capably defended island in the world." But because of its strategic importance, both the Japanese and Americans knew that the victor of the war must control this island.

George Wahlen landed on Iwo Jima on D-day, February 19, 1945. His unit suffered more than 100% casualties when counting the replacement troops. He spent 12 horrific days on this barely habitable island, and during that time, saved the lives of countless men, all while enduring two painful injuries. After his third debilitating injury, he crawled 50 yards to treat another wounded Marine before finally being evacuated.

His incredible acts of bravery, despite heavy enemy shelling, resulted in his earning the Medal of Honor.

As many combat veterans, George has endured a lifetime of lingering injuries and tortuous memories. But as a Medal of Honor recipient, he continues to deflect any personal praise, choosing instead to remind us of the heroes who never returned. He has dedicated his life to serving veterans, honoring their sacrifices, and reminding us of their contribution to our way of life. He is the veteran's veteran, having served almost every branch of the military at one point or another during his life. His story is not just the story of an American hero, which he undoubtedly is. His story is one of inspiration and motivation for all of us who came from humble beginnings, and made the best with what God has given us.

George Wahlen is a man whom I am honored to call a friend. I pay tribute to him, and to all veterans, past and present, who have sacrificed on our behalf, that we might be protected from the evil forces that continue to threaten us.

PREFACE

"Where dark tides billow in the ocean,
A wink-shaped isle of mighty fame
Guards the gate to our Empire,
Iwo Jima is its name."

—*Japanese Children's Song*

The battle for Iwo Jima is recognized as the most costly American battle of World War II. General Holland M. Smith, Commander of the Expeditionary Troops, described it as "the most savage and the most costly battle in the history of the Marine Corps." Indeed, it had few parallels in modern military annals, and post-battle analysts said, "Taking Iwo Jima was like throwing human flesh against reinforced concrete."

This barely inhabitable island lay 670 miles almost due south of Tokyo. It had less strategic value to the Japanese than psychological, but its value to the Americans was both offensive and defensive. Iwo Jima was seen as a means of intensifying the bombing on the Japanese mainland. Additionally, the capture of Iwo Jima offered a safe haven for B-29s returning from their bomb runs on Japan.

Had the U.S. attacked the island a year earlier, it would have taken less than a week to conquer because the Japanese were ill prepared to defend it then. After months of incessant U.S. bombing (beginning in July of 1944), Japanese commanders devised a brilliant subterranean defense network that nearly succeeded in weakening America's will to fight. With so many casualties, repercussions from bereaved families after this battle forced American leaders to rethink future engagement strategies. The memory of the Japanese army's desperate determination to fight a losing battle at Iwo Jima weighed heavily on the minds of U.S. leaders in the decision to drop the atomic bomb.

The human toll was enormous at Iwo Jima, as one-third of all Marine casualties in WWII happened there. For the U.S., 6,821 sons, husbands, brothers, and fathers breathed their final breath on the island, while another 21,865 were wounded in the endeavor to wrest it from the enemy. It was the only time in WWII that U.S. casualties exceeded that of the Japanese, and more men died during this conflict than died on the D-day invasion of Normandy. Not since Gettysburg had more men died during a single battle.

For the Japanese, all but 1,083 of the estimated 21,000 defenders died on Iwo Jima, and most of those captured were conscripted Korean laborers. Many Japanese soldiers opted to blow themselves apart by detonating a grenade in their stomach instead of being captured. The enemy's insistence on death over capture further disconnected the Marines from humanity, ultimately leading to a profound number of battle fatigue cases. More than 2,500 men suffered from this combat malady during the battle, but many also suffered severe mental illness that continued throughout their lives.

As in any war, heroes are born amid the battle's din. The uninformed might say the battlefield makes heroes of cowards because the only option is to fight or die, but self-preservation must never be confused with heroism. These men were not motivated solely by a fear of death, although in battle, that fear is ever present for all warriors. What sets heroes apart is their overwhelming need to do their duty in spite of otherwise paralyzing fear. In many cases, what they feared most was disappointing a comrade, shrinking in the face of danger, or not doing enough to save a friend.

Some of these heroes survived to tell their tale, while others are memorialized by the comrades who survived them. During the 36 days of the Iwo Jima conflict, an unprecedented 27 men were distinguished with the Medal of Honor, the nation's highest honor for valor. Of those 27 recipients, just 14 survived the battle; 13 were honored posthumously. Those who survived proudly wear their medals in part to honor their fallen comrades. These genuine heroes often renounce the hero moniker and insist that they are no more courageous, no more dauntless, and no more gallant than the buddies with whom they served. However, the truth about their character resonates in the Chinese proverb: heroes create circumstances and circumstances create heroes.

This book describes the experiences of one such person: Pharmacist Mate 2nd Class George E. Wahlen, who was one of the few Medal of Honor recipients from the Iwo Jima campaign. Through the providence of the Almighty, he survived 13 days of violent, brutal combat, saving countless Marines before finally being evacuated after his third, most debilitating wound.

The case of George Wahlen shows that heroes can emerge from obscurity. He grew up in rural Utah and was influenced by the poverty of the depression-era economy in the 1930s. Devoutly loyal to his parents, he inherited his father's strong will. Desperate not to be left out of the war, he created the circumstance that permitted him to be drafted into the service. He was denied the chance to serve as an aircraft mechanic for the Navy, though he had pre-war experience servicing aircraft. He begrudgingly trained as a corpsman, and was one of only a handful of men who volunteered to be attached to a Marine combat unit.

Unlike most units that trained for several months on average, his unit trained together for over a year before jumping into the savage and unrelenting combat on Iwo Jima. The year together created a bond of unfailing devotion among these brothers in arms who proudly became known as Fox Company, 2nd Battalion, 26th Regiment of the 5th Marine Division. Of those 250 men of Fox Company who landed on Iwo Jima on D-day, February 19, 1945, only a handful walked off the island.

His unit was distinguished in many ways. Fox Company produced two Medal of Honor recipients (Franklin E. Sigler and George E. Wahlen), four Navy Cross recipients (Frank Caldwell, John C. Folsom, Martin L. Gelshenen, George L. Long), four Silver Star, seven Bronze Star, six Letters of Commendation, and 230 Purple Heart recipients. This astonishing medal count is but a snapshot of the countless acts of bravery and courage not officially recognized with a medal.

Although many have written brief accounts of how George earned his medal, this is the first and only authorized published account detailing his historic feats. It not only highlights George's heroic efforts, but also those of his Fox Company brothers who were equally gallant in battle.

This work was completed as a labor of love for all veterans who have served their country. In particular, it stands as a tribute to all men who served this country during World War II. May we never forget their sacrifices on our behalf.

Chapter One

D-day, February 19, 1945

Hunkered down on the island of Iwo Jima, George Wahlen and his unit, ("F" Company, 2nd Battalion, 26th Marines, 5th Marine Division) waited anxiously for orders to advance. Powerful explosions rocked the ground, spewing the gritty volcanic sand skyward in geyser-like fountains. Enemy rifle fire whizzed menacingly overhead, and all too often these projectiles collided silently with a Marine unable to avoid its path. The concentrated barrage of mortars, artillery and rifle fire continued to pour on the hapless stream of Marines coming ashore. George could only watch helplessly as an interminable half hour passed.

With nothing to gain but death by staying on the beach, the Marines began their push inland. Seeing the waves of Marines making their move,

A Marine who gave his life for his country

the Japanese were determined to keep the Americans on the open beach where they were easier targets. But one by one, the Marines advanced further inland and found limited protection in large shell holes from the Navy's earlier bombardment.

As he kept his head down and watched the action, George saw a platoon runner crawl up to the lieutenant, keeping his body low against the ground.

"I lost my rifle," the young Marine said in a shaky voice.

The lieutenant looked at the Marine and motioned toward the beach now scattered with fallen Marines. "That's OK. There's plenty of dead men over here. Take one of their rifles."

George watched as the weaponless Marine crawled 20 yards away to a fellow Marine whose body lay motionless, face down in the sand. When he tapped his shoulder, he got no response, so he pushed his shoulder to try to roll him over on his back. George watched silently, hoping the young Marine would work faster, since the shower of bullets and shrapnel continued flying about. As the Marine struggled to roll the lifeless body over on his back, from a distance, George could see as the startled young Marine stared at the bloody bullet hole between the man's eyes and a pool of coagulated blood that had clumped in the sand.

George watched the young Marine turn white with terror, then in an instant, compose himself. He quickly grabbed the Garand rifle from the lifeless Marine's hands, then retreated, lizard-like, back to a sandy depression near George.

That was the moment when it really hit George. This was not a training exercise. It was that instant he realized that someone was in fact trying to kill him, and that he indeed might be killed.

CHAPTER TWO

BIRTH TO BOOT CAMP

"God is training up his heroes and when they appear, the world will wonder where they came from."   *—C.S. Lewis*

Before George Wahlen joined the fighting ranks of the Marines, his life started as many had in the desert state of Utah.

Devoid of tall trees, grass, or most anything lush and green, his birth city of Fairmont consisted of unincorporated farming properties several miles west of Ogden. It was a barren looking place sandwiched between the Wasatch Range to the east and the brine-fly infested Great Salt Lake to the west. Not even the most optimistic Utah farmer would have considered this choice farming property, but it

George Wahlen as a young child

was home to his parents, Albert and Doris Wahlen, who lived rent-free in a small house on property owned by Doris' parents. In 1924, the newlyweds were eking out a living by helping maintain the farm.

When George was born on August 8, 1924, Doris was surrounded by her mother—and a number of interested family members—as she gave birth to her first baby. Without a physician available, the group sprang into action when the infant was unable to breathe. Just minutes old, they resuscitated the baby by dipping his small body into tubs of water—one filled with hot, one with cold—to shock the baby into taking his first breath. Minutes later, George was breathing normally as his new parents and grandparents let out a collective sigh of relief. The initial panic left them joking with each other to release the tension.

The Wahlens, like many Utah farmers, struggled to make ends meet. The parched soil required constant irrigation to keep the crops from baking in the desert sun. During the depression years, they moved to a small house behind the home of George's Grandmother Wahlen in Ogden, Utah.

As a child, George and his father would go out after dark in the adjacent lawns, crawling on their hands and knees searching for earthworms or "night crawlers." The worms were popular bait among local fisherman and could be found abundantly in surrounding lawns.

George painted a sign and hung it on a fencepost in front of his home, advertising his squirming fishbait to would-be anglers. With George in the retail worm business, his ability to play baseball with his friends was limited, a constant frustration to him. But it wasn't all for naught. The result of his summer-long enterprise was a substantial savings account and a much needed boost to his family's income.

George gave his money to his father for safekeeping, but it didn't land in a bank. George's father had lost his life's savings during the collapse of the banking system in 1929, so he stashed the money in a tin can and hid it in the crawl space of George's uncle who lived next door.

The Wahlens spent 12 years in that small house, working to save their money. In 1936 they had saved enough money for a down payment on a $1,200 house located on ten-acres of land less than a mile from the home where George was born.

Beginning in 1930, George attended Pingree and Lewis Elementary Schools, Wilson Lane School, and Weber High School. He developed a

George's younger twin brothers, Gene and Jack Wahlen

George in a class photo at Wilson Lane School circa 1934

reputation as a tenacious 110-pound brawler. He won his weight division as a wrestler, and he was a regular participant in boxing matches staged at local drive-ins until he broke his hand during a match.

Despite his size, he was a fierce competitor on the Weber High School junior varsity football team. He played halfback during his freshman and sophomore years, but his size became a problem his varsity year. At the start of his senior season, George sat on the bench for the first two practice games. After the second game, he promptly marched into the coach's office, thrust his uniform on the floor and barked, "Give it to someone who you'll let play." He stormed out of the office and never played again.

By 1940, the world had already seen the Nazis seize control of most of Europe, and the rumblings of war were growing louder with each passing month. The European war hit home the hardest on September 16, 1940, when President Franklin D. Roosevelt signed the Selective Service Act, enacting the first peacetime draft. As George and many other boys contemplated their future, it became increasingly evident that the United States was going to war, and that the rapidly growing industrial war complex would offer new hope for employment.

In November 1941, George was in his senior year at Weber High School. Wanting to learn a trade, he asked his father to let him drop out of high school to enroll in an aircraft engine mechanic's course at Utah Agricultural College in Logan, Utah. If he were accepted, he would receive a $15 per month stipend while taking the course.

Like many parents, Mr. Wahlen knew that eventually George would be drafted, but reluctantly agreed to allow him to quit school. The very next day, George drove his 1928 Chevrolet to Logan and enrolled in the aircraft mechanic course.

School was to begin on Monday, December 8, 1941. The day before school started George canvassed the neighborhoods around the Logan campus, looking for a room to rent. His mind was so focused on his immediate task that he was oblivious to the historic events unfolding at Pearl Harbor that fateful Sunday morning.

When he arrived at school the next morning, he immediately learned of the Japanese attack. He was caught up in the emotions of shock and anger expressed by his classmates. Most of the students and faculty huddled around the radio, straining to hear President Roosevelt call for a declaration of war against the Empire of Japan.

With a new, more clarified purpose, George studied hard to complete his course work. Most weekends he would drive to his parents' home to do laundry, sleep in a comfortable bed, and eat familiar food.

After only a few months at school, a recruiter from the Army Air Corps offered George a sergeant's rating upon the completion of his schooling. George was thrilled. Not only was he excited to make a contribution to the war, he was also eager to receive a respectable pay.

At his first opportunity, George returned home for the weekend, hoping that the months away from home had increased his father's willingness to give him more freedom. Although not fully confident his father would agree, he had nothing to lose by asking him to sign the enlistment papers. George explained that the Army Air Corps wanted to recruit him, but before he could explain the details, his father pushed the enlistment papers back to George and said, "I didn't let you quit school just for you to go into the service."

Dejected, George returned to Logan that evening and mulled over his options. Despite his strong desire to enlist, he could see no benefit in disobeying his father. He wasn't accustomed to acting contrary to his father's wishes, and doing so seemed unthinkable.

George continued his training, and after six months graduated from the course. He was immediately hired at Hill Field near Ogden, which was only a short drive from his parents' home. George was hired as part of a flight test section that assessed each plane for airworthiness.

Hill Field bustled with the roar of incoming planes and was a critical part of the U.S. military build up. Shipments of planes, parts, and other materials arrived round the clock, as the Army Air Corps was frantic to build up its inventory. In addition, many planes received a special winterizing treatment there, prior to being sent directly to Russia.

George worked hard and earned the confidence of his coworkers. After eight months on the job, he was promoted to crew chief and became responsible for managing five other mechanics. As a team, they worked diligently to keep up with the demands of the increasing number of aircraft.

At 17 years old, George was proud of his own accomplishments and with the relatively high level of responsibility he was given at a young age. He savored the surge of confidence it engendered and was awed at the faith and trust he had gained from both his superiors and subordinates. Concerned about disappointing them, George was determined to maintain their trust by doing his job the best he could.

George's desire to join the war intensified when he turned 18 that August (1942). Each day the newspaper articles featured new enlistees and their exotic destinations for training or deployment. Many of George's friends had already been activated, causing him even more frustration with his father's insistence that he not enlist. Although he understood why his father was trying to protect him, it didn't deter his commitment to find a way to comply with his father's demands, yet still get into the service.

George continued to work at Hill Field, living at home and feeling as though the world was passing him by. In June 1943, he learned of a friend who had volunteered for the draft. He thought long about this tactic, reasoning that it could prevent upsetting his father, yet still accomplish his aim of joining the service. He asked himself "how could my Dad argue with a forced induction notice?"

On June 11, he drove his '28 Chevrolet down Highway 89, past the Utah State Capitol and to the east bench where the University of Utah and Fort Douglas shared the foothills.

Fort Douglas served as the headquarters for the Ninth Service Command and was a reception center for hordes of incoming servicemen and women. The locale's winding, tree lined streets and old red sandstone buildings quickly gave way to the utilitarian structures under construction. George parked his car and looked for direction signs guiding him to the building for new inductees.

George was confident that his skills would make him a sought-after commodity among any branch of the service. He went first to the officer representing the Army Air Force office, thinking his formal training and experience as a crew chief at Hill Field would translate into a higher rank. His hopes were dashed, though, when the officer explained that the Army Air Force had no vacancies and didn't anticipate needing new inductees in the near future. George was instructed to go down the hall because the Navy maintained a fleet of planes, and his skills might be of use. George cocked his head to the side and shrugged his shoulders in agreement.

Thanking the officer for the advice he walked anxiously down the hall to the Navy office. George again explained his work experience and desire to work on airplanes. But this was an induction office and not a recruiting office, so George's sales pitch fell on deaf ears. Because George was offering to be an inductee, he was in no position to negotiate his assignment.

George was forced to rely on the Navy's common sense when it came to his assignment. Confident that his training would not go to waste, he sat down and signed the induction papers on the spot.

The officer shook George's hand and congratulated him on being an official member of the United States Navy. George was instructed to get his affairs in order, as he could expect his induction notice within a few days. George smiled and left the building, thinking he had just outsmarted the system, and more important, his father.

CHAPTER THREE

SAILOR TO MARINE

As the American war machine continued its dramatic build up, young men poured into train and bus stations throughout the country. Ogden's Union Station was no different, as soon-to-be soldiers, sailors, and Marines tugged their luggage and duffel bags into the large, cathedral-size room to bid farewell to family and friends. Some boys, trying to mask their apprehension, donned brave, smiling faces. But most were leaving home for the first time and could not mask the fear of their potentially perilous future.

It was June 18, 1943, just eight days after signing his induction papers. George nervously said good-bye to his parents and twin brothers Gene and Jack, then climbed aboard the southbound train destined for Southern California. The whistle blew as the train lunged and jerked its way beyond the train station. George sat silently watching as the mountains, street signs, and businesses passed by him. Within minutes, the familiar landmarks he had known since childhood faded into the horizon.

The train made stops in Salt Lake City and Las Vegas before reaching its destination, the Naval Training Center in San Diego. George kept to himself during the long hours on the train, replaying in his mind the whirlwind of events that had brought him to this moment eight days later.

He recalled when his induction notice arrived in the mail. His father's face was emotionless, neither creasing into a smile or a frown, as he looked at the official-looking letter sitting on the kitchen table. George hadn't revealed to his father that he had traveled to Salt Lake City to volunteer for the draft. He was still confident that his father didn't know, despite the suspiciously short span between receiving his notice and having to report to basic training.

That notice was the reason George sat on the train for the long and bumpy ride to San Diego. As they arrived, George spotted a sharply dressed sailor waiting to escort the new recruits and inductees to a bus parked nearby.

As soon as he stepped off the bus, George endured the ample portions of humiliation, boredom, and physical exertion that he had expected from basic training. Drill instructors yelled at sailors for not listening, not working fast enough, or working too fast. Inductees were demeaned with such appellations as "ladies" and "girls," both cutting epithets that were sure to elicit snickers from others who were lucky enough to avoid the reprimand.

Days after arriving, his group sat in a large classroom to take an aptitude and IQ test, which provided a welcomed respite from the marching and other physical training maneuvers. Even though George hated the yelling and degradation that accompanied the physical training, he tried to keep quiet and do what he was told, fearing the sudden castigation that accompanied any mistake, misstep, or mishap. Each day he dutifully marched on the parade field, performed endless calisthenics, and then marched some more.

His marching was so awkward that a chief petty officer took him aside and gave him individual marching lessons. While his fellow inductees were in their barracks relaxing for the night, George was out on the grinder (parade field) practicing his left-right-left. Night

Taking aptitude and IQ tests was a welcomed diversion for some

after night, from six to nine each evening, he hauled his seabags, hoping to find the cure for his two left feet. After four weeks of practice, George managed to pass inspection during his marches, but he still could only keep time by mumbling the cadence under his breath and keenly watching the feet of those in front of him.

Graduation day brought news of his next training assignment. He was shocked to learn that instead of going to aircraft mechanic's school, he was being sent to hospital corps school. Initially confused, he later grew angry about his surprising assignment. He tromped over to the commander's office to protest his duty assignment, but his plea to be transferred was ignored. In desperation, George hitched a ride up the road to the Hospital Corps School in Balboa Park to visit with the instructor. He tracked down a warrant officer in charge of the school and asked for permission to speak.

"Go ahead, son," the fatherly officer replied.

George measured his words, hoping not to appear too desperate. "I believe the Navy has made a mistake by assigning me to corpsman school."

*George upon graduation from
Navy basic training in 1943*

"And why is that?" the officer asked in a puzzled tone.

"Well," George said confidently, "I've spent the last year working as the chief of a flight test section at Hill Field in Utah. I'm a darn good aircraft mechanic, and the Army Air Corps promoted me to that position because I was pretty good at it. I don't want to be a corpsman; I can be more help to the Navy if I'm fixing planes."

The officer smiled and thought a few

seconds before replying, "I'll tell you what." He paused, and George looked up, eagerly hoping he had succeeded in convincing him to change his assignment.

"If you do real well in this school, I'll see what I can do to get you transferred." George quickly shook the officer's hand and said, "Thank you, sir. I promise I'll work real hard." George was so happy he nearly tripped on a chair as he scrambled out of the office.

Clinging to the words of hope offered by the school's top officer, George reported for duty, determined to leave no doubt about how well he could do. He studied each subject intently—often staying up until midnight just to make sure he did "real well" on his exams. After eight weeks of intense coursework, George finished in the top 25 in a class of more than 400 corpsmen.

The day of graduation, George took his graduation certificate straightway to the director's office and asked for permission to see the officer again.

When George entered the officer's small office, he waited to be authorized to speak. Then the medical officer looked up at him.

"Sir," George spoke politely, "if you remember, we talked when I first came here, and you promised that if I did real well here, you would get me transferred to an aircraft maintenance unit. Well, as you can see, I was in the top 25 of my class." The officer looked at the certificate; he half-grinned as he peered over the paper that George had given him. As he looked up, he was both amused and bewildered that George expected an immediate change of his orders. The officer sat quietly at his desk, then cleared his throat before replying, "I know you want to be an airplane mechanic, but we need good men in the hospital corps too." The officer then promptly replied, "You're dismissed."

George walked from the office and stood motionless in the hallway, still holding the certificate in his hand. He was overwhelmed, confused, and dumbfounded as the finality of the officer's pronouncement still rung in his ears. As he walked out of the building, he knew he was stuck being a corpsman, and there was nothing he or anyone else could do about it.

George was assigned to work in a medical ward at the Naval Hospital in Balboa Park. Like all corpsmen, he changed bedpans, cleaned floors, and, worst of all, took orders from female nurses. He was unaccustomed to being subordinate to a woman. Throughout his life, he had never answered to a female (other than his mother) and felt it demeaning to do so. Such attitudes were characteristic of many American men at that time, and continued long after World War II.

George, frustrated with his job, became increasingly dissatisfied with each passing week. His only consolation came when he learned that as an apprentice corpsman, he could be promoted if he passed an examination. A promotion meant an increase in pay, which was powerful motivation, since the job itself held no reward for him. If he couldn't change what he was doing, at least he could be paid more to do it. He asked three other apprentice corpsmen why they hadn't taken the test, and they warned him that passing the test would result in being sent to sea, or worse yet, being assigned to the Marines and a combat unit. That didn't matter to George, though. He decided to take the test and accept the consequences. Anything was better than what he was doing.

Fearing that George would be promoted ahead of them, all four corpsmen took the test together. Within weeks they were all promoted to hospital apprentice, first class, which meant they were doing the same job for a few dollars more per month. The next month, George completed another examination and was again promoted—this time to pharmacist's mate, third class. He again made a few dollars more for doing the same thing, day after day, week after week.

Still, George did find some benefits from his tedious and, to him, demeaning duties. Working in the ward gave him the opportunity to speak with many wounded Marines. Prior to volunteering for the Navy, George had contemplated joining the Marines, but his father minced no words as he exclaimed, "Like hell you will!" He gave no other reason, other than it was not an option. George didn't give it much serious consideration thereafter.

Lately, though, George often asked Marine patients what it was like for Navy corpsmen assigned to the Marines, and the stories they told him were encouraging. George was growing increasingly impatient with his duty assignment, and was desperate to change his circumstances. If corpsmen were treated as the equals of the Marines in their units, he would seriously consider his option of being assigned to the Marines. So he kept asking questions. He was happy to learn that corpsmen trained alongside the Marines and were respected and admired for the job they accomplished.

George seriously considered volunteering for the Marines, but couldn't quite bring himself to actually make that decision. It was a confrontation with a nurse that convinced him to finally make up his mind.

He had just finished a long shift when the head nurse started arguing with George about his work. "Didn't I ask you an hour ago to empty those bedpans?" she huffed. George, though seething inside, didn't offer a reply. "If I tell you to do something, you had better do it. Do you want me to send you to the Marines?" George bristled at the notion that she could punish him, and he abruptly shot back, "Sister, you're not sending me anywhere." He walked off the ward and immediately walked across the street to the master-of-arms shack, where he could volunteer for a Marine assignment.

Eager to accept volunteers, the petty officer readily admitted George and instructed him to pack his seabag and report for duty at 0800 hours the next day. George smiled, having claimed a victory over his distasteful duties, and above all, over the charge nurse who sought to threaten him. He gave the petty officer a sharp salute and went directly to his barracks. Once again having shaped his own destiny, George was ready for his adventure to begin.

CHAPTER FOUR

TRAINING TO TRAINING

E ven for sunlit San Diego, the day seemed even more brilliant than normal as George reported for duty at 0800 hours with his seabag in tow. Although he was apprehensive when he thought about the unknown demands of the Marines, his anxiety was miniscule compared to the giddiness he felt to leave behind bedpans, mops and above all, bossy nurses.

George was one of fourteen new corpsmen reporting for duty. Of the group, eleven wore white uniforms bearing the word "BRIG" written in big black letters across their backs. These men had been jailed for various infractions and had opted for an infantry assignment rather than remain incarcerated in the brig. George and his new cohorts filed onto a bus that was headed southward to Camp Elliott— a relatively small training base in San Diego County. Camp Elliott served as the advanced training site and headquarters for the West Coast elements of the Fleet Marine Force.[1] The landscape offered a unique combination of gently rolling hills and steep mountain slopes that were ideal for infantry conditioning as well as weapons and field maneuver training.

Entering the gates at Camp Elliott, George thought of his own basic training experience, and couldn't see much difference in how the Marines trained their recruits. He watched as Marine prisoners with shaven heads were "double-timed" across the parade field by Marine MPs (Military Police). George and his fellow corpsmen recruits were hustled off the bus and given instructions about the next seven weeks of training and indoctrination that would shape them into Marine field medical corpsmen.

After stowing their seabags for safekeeping, they were rushed into a tent, where they stood in line waiting to be issued their new Marine uniforms—

sage green 3-pocket tunics and standard Marine issue camouflage trousers. [2]

As they carried their new uniforms with both arms, they advanced to the next room to receive new footwear, or what Marines called "boondockers." Each man called out his shoe size, and the supply sergeant would call out the shoe size to another Marine waiting behind the counter. Within seconds, a new pair of boots would be slammed on the table, and the waiting corpsman would scoop them up and move outside.

Training at Camp Elliott was more difficult than George had expected. He ran obstacle courses, hiked with full gear, and endured endless marching on the parade field. Initially, the training was so strenuous that George asked himself, "What did I get myself into?" But as he became accustomed to the pace, his confidence grew stronger, and he found he could keep up with his comrades.

George and the other corpsmen were expected to learn how to use all types of weapons, including rifles, mortars, and grenades. In addition to the infantry training, many of their days were spent in the classroom learning how to dress shrapnel wounds, splint a broken bone, or treat an open belly wound. These skills would then be practiced in simulated live-fire battle training.

The training was intense and demanding. George was proud to be in peak physical condition after finishing his training at the end of seven weeks. He didn't have long to wait before learning his next assignment, which was at Camp Pendleton, just a few miles up the California coast.

Because the Marines were primarily responsible for the execution of the Pacific war, it was necessary to find an expansive tract of land to train an extraordinarily large number of Marine recruits. Although Camp Elliott was ideal for small-unit training, it lacked sufficient space to host the division-sized training exercises that would be needed to take on the formidable Japanese defenses.

In March of 1942, the Navy purchased approximately 130,000 acres called the Rancho Santa Margarita y Las Flores, located east of Oceanside between Los Angeles and San Diego. In September of 1942, construction proceeded at a furious pace. Within months, the sleepy cattle ranch was converted into a bustling military installation capable of training and transporting immense numbers of Marines.[3]

Sea of tents at the newly constructed Camp Pendleton,
just outside Oceanside, California

George was assigned to the new 5th Marine Division. 5th Division Head-quarters officially began operation at Camp Pendleton on December 1, 1943, when military equipment and men began streaming into the camp. On January 21, 1944, the Division was officially activated.[4]

When George arrived at Camp Pendleton in March, the 5th Marine Division and its respective units were still being organized. The core of the 5th Division was organized around the battle-wise veterans who had seen action on Guadalcanal, Bougainville, and Tarawa. Some were from Marine Raider and ParaMarine battalions that were disbanded in late 1943. Many of these experienced troops were transferred to the new 5th Division.[5]

Combining these experienced Marines with new ones fresh from boot training, initially created some friction. The first day at Camp Pendleton, Corpsman Peter Karegeannes was placing his seabag on his bunk, when another young Marine realized that he was sharing his barracks with a sail-or. The brassy new Marine began taunting the corpsman and derided him with the final insult "chancre mechanic." The veteran sergeant, who had seen combat at Guadalcanal, heard the comment and jumped to the defense of the corpsman. Pointing his finger at the open-eyed young Marine, the sergeant barked back saying, "Once you get into combat, you're going to regret ever talking bad about the corpsmen. When you're hit, and you call for a corpsman, you better hope he doesn't ignore you." He promptly assigned the young Marine to a week's worth of extra duty.[6]

Once bunks had been assigned, the company gathered as a unit for the first time on the parade field. George was assigned to Fox Company, 2nd Battalion of the 26th Marine Regiment. His unit was introduced to the commanding officer, Captain Frank C. Caldwell, who was a remnant of a disbanded Marine parachute regiment.

At 23 years old, Caldwell was one of the youngest captains in the United States Marine Corps.[7] He had spent over a year in New Caledonia in the Southwest Pacific, where his parachute regiment trained, but never jumped into combat.

1st Lieutenant Frank C. Caldwell when serving with the 1st Marine Parachute Battalion in 1943

When the parachutists were demobilized, the men were scattered throughout the Marine Corps. Caldwell spent an entire month on "R & R," but was eventually transferred to the newly organized 5th Division at Camp Pendleton.

Caldwell hailed from Spartanburg, South Carolina, and southern inflections and colorful words peppered his language. He was well-liked by both his subordinate officers and NCOs, and was committed to having his company in peak physical condition.

George had just come from three long months of Field Medical Corpsman Training and was confident in his conditioning. He wasn't concerned when he learned his company was ordered to go on a twenty-mile march. He learned quickly, however, what Captain Caldwell's idea of conditioning was all about.

Having earned the rank of pharmacist's mate third class in the Navy, which translated into a three-stripe sergeant in the Marines, George was the ranking corpsman of his company. Captain Caldwell assigned him to remain at the front of the column with the men of Headquarters Company. The remaining corpsmen were assigned to fall back with their platoons. As each platoon hiked up the mountain, a corpsman would bring up the rear to watch for stragglers.

As the hike progressed, the company of Marines became spread out over several hundred yards. At the end of each hour, the C.O. (Commanding Officer) ordered a ten-minute rest for everyone except George. At each break, George hoofed it back to the end of the column to inquire about any medical concerns from each corpsman. Running as quickly as his rubbery legs would allow, hour after hour, George made it to the end of the column and returned just as the company began moving out again. At two in the morning, George and all his weary Marine comrades trudged back into their bunks. But George wasn't finished yet, as he and the other corpsmen treated blisters and other foot ailments for another hour before finally dragging themselves to bed.

Two columns of weary Marines returning from a daylong forced march

The long marches and other training exercises gave George a chance to meet the other corpsmen in his regiment. At roll and mail calls, he learned the names of all his fellow corpsmen and the Marines in his platoon. It wasn't long before friendships were forged that would create bonds they often described as "closer than brothers."

George struck up a friendship with Edward "Eddie" Monjaras of Cheyenne, Wyoming. Eddie, of Mexican descent, stood about five feet, eight inches tall. He wasn't as thin or wiry as George, but wasn't pudgy either. His coarse, black hair and bright white teeth were a startling contrast to his slightly darkened brown skin. Every corpsman liked Eddie and enjoyed being around him. He wasn't boisterous or loud, but his quick, white smile was endearing. Eddie was a loyal friend and found ways to protect George and other corpsmen during inspections. Although Eddie was in the 2nd platoon and George in the 1st, they both spent a great deal of their free time together, playing basketball or other organized games.

A few weeks after George and the rest of his unit had settled in, Corpsman Robert "Bob" DeGeus was assigned to Fox Company. Bob was a diminutive young man, not more than 125 pounds, and stood about five feet, eight inches tall. Being a latecomer meant that Bob was not quickly assimilated into the social structure of the company. He was left out of most unit activities and spent his time alone while everyone else was on liberty. George befriended Bob and invited him to take a liberty trip to Santa Monica to visit his Aunt Lillian and Uncle Edward "Eddie" Hobbs.

Aunt Lil and Uncle Eddie owned a modest, three-bedroom home in a quiet neigh-

Edward "Eddie" Monjaras from Cheyenne, Wyoming

borhood in this yet-to-be-discovered sleepy beach town. George and Eddie—and later Bob—found it much easier to hitch a ride up the Pacific Coast Highway when they wore their uniforms.

Aunt Lil had no children, and George and his younger brothers were her only nephews. She loved to dote on George, Eddie, and Bob, and she would treat them to homemade meals, clean sheets, and all the comforts of being at home. She was a terrific cook, but it didn't matter whether the trio of famished corpsmen were hungry, they dove into their food because anything was better than military chow.

Living next door to George's aunt was a gorgeous brunette with a stunning smile and warm dark eyes. She was also confined to a wheelchair. George never learned her name, or the reason she needed the wheelchair, but her limited mobility meant that she didn't get out of her house much. The wheelchair was not a deterrent for Eddie. Each time he arrived at Aunt Lil's, his first priority was to go next door to see her. The two struck up a friendly relationship, and they began writing to each other. Eddie took advantage of every opportunity to go on liberty with George to see Aunt Lil. But after a few trips, George realized it wasn't Aunt Lil's cooking that kept Eddie coming back.

Hitchhiking for a ride southbound to Camp Pendelton seemed a little more difficult than finding a ride north to Los Angeles. With many men in uniform heading in the same direction, it reduced the pool of potential cars willing to pick up a stranger. It also may have seemed longer because the fun was nearing an end, and the next liberty seemed to be years away.

Robert "Bob" DeGeus from Eaton Rapids, Michigan

Back at camp, the training regimen continued at a fierce pace, and all
men were expected to work hard and complete their training. George and
his fellow corpsmen were not given lighter assignments than the rest of
their platoon; they were expected to be prepared to make a contribution to
their fighting unit. Unlike their Army counterparts, Navy corpsmen trained
alongside the Marines in their combat training. Corpsmen knew how to
effectively use carbines, grenades, Browning Automatic Rifles (BARs), machine guns, and most every weapon generally used by a rifle platoon in the
Marines. Corpsmen also participated in demolitions training, and assault
and tank-infantry tactics as well. Each night would rumble and crack with
the sounds of discharging weapons throughout Camp Pendleton as training intensified. Within weeks, the 5th Division was quickly developing into
a cohesive unit of fighting men.

Just as each man was beginning to feel confident about his conditioning and weapons proficiency, officers would up the ante by adding more
complex tasks to the training. Night after night, Marines would crawl over

Marines and corpsmen trained side by side. Here they practice their aim at
Camp Pendleton's firing range

simulated battlefields with bullets whizzing over their heads in live ammunition battle simulations. Everyone, including corpsmen, were involved in the training, since they needed to practice treating simulated wounds and evacuating their "casualties" to the aid stations in the rear.

As the weeks progressed, platoons and companies began integrating their training at the battalion level; then battalions were joining together for regimental exercises. Everyone knew their role in the scheme of an effective unit, and by late spring, the units were training for amphibious landings.

These landings were dangerous, and officers had little patience for horseplay. Training was methodical and began with Marines practicing on land-based dummy landing craft, climbing up and down rope nets. This task was harder than it would seem and became increasingly dangerous with full gear and rifle. Stepping down the rope net required timing and strength, as each Marine had to avoid stepping on the man below, while being wary of having his hand squashed by the man above. For the first few days, Marines could be heard cursing when someone above smashed their hand or kicked their head.

The next task was to learn how to properly disembark from a large transport ship into an LCVP (Landing Craft, Vehicles and Personnel). The disembarking process became even more complicated in heavy seas, as the ship and the LCVP lunged and rocked with the crashing waves. After weeks of amphibious landing exercises, Marines grew weary of the repetition and became proficient at getting in and out of their LCVP.

With no notion of when they would be sent into battle, the Marines concentrated on improving their conditioning. Physical fitness was critical to building a successful fighting unit. Daily calisthenics, obstacle courses, and forced marches without rest periods remained a vital part of the conditioning routine.

As the physical demands increased, so did the Marines' injuries and ailments. George learned to treat multiple ailments, but mostly he treated feet; blisters and foot injuries were the most common affliction after a long march. Corpsmen also treated cold and flu symptoms, which somehow seemed to escalate before each anticipated forced march.

George realized that as a corpsman, he had few treatment options when an ailing Marine asked for help. When first aid wasn't an option, the usual remedy was a little pink tablet called an APC (aspirin, phenacetin and caffeine). Like every other corpsman, George was issued a large bottle of APCs and gave them out for everything ranging from fallen arches to headaches. If the corpsmen couldn't solve the problem, the senior corpsman was called, or, if warranted, the battalion surgeon took the case.[8]

Leathernecks quickly learned that the corpsmen were good people to know, especially because they had the authority to assign Marines to light duty or sick call. On one occasion before a long hike, two Marines approached George and begged to avoid the hike, claiming their blisters were not yet healed. George knew they had healed, but their persistence convinced George to acquiesce. He reluctantly authorized light duty. The two Marines relished their light duty while the rest of the outfit endured a grueling forced march. That evening, when Fox Company dragged themselves back to their bunks, one of the excused Marines laughed at George and said, "If you weren't so stupid, you wouldn't have to go on those hikes either."

Angered, George went directly to his First Sergeant and reported their plot to avoid the march. For the next few weeks the unhappy Marines spent their free time filling potholes in the company's dirt street.

By spring, George had earned several weeks of liberty, and he eagerly took the time to go back to Utah to see his family. This was his first chance to be home since he was inducted more than a year earlier.

George arrived at Union Station in downtown Ogden and stepped off the train, proudly wearing his Marine uniform. He enjoyed wearing both the Navy and Marine uniforms when he went out visiting friends and family. Usually he wore his Marine uniform to confuse those who thought he was in the Navy. But a nosy neighbor, distrusting George's alternating attire, called in the military police. One afternoon, an Army MP knocked on the Wahlen's door demanding to see Navy Corpsman George E. Wahlen. George happened to be wearing his Marine uniform that day, and the MP demanded an explanation of why he was wearing an unauthorized uniform.

George smiled nervously as he explained to the uninformed soldier that he was a Navy corpsman attached to the Marines and was authorized to wear both uniforms. The MP grew impatient with George's explanation. He prepared to arrest George, and transport him to his superior officers for them to sort out the situation. After a heated conversation, lasting almost 30 minutes, George produced sufficient documentation to satisfy the

MP. He drove away leaving George and his parents to breathe a nervous sigh of relief. From that point on, George only wore his Navy uniform to prevent any further problems with the law.

By mid-June, the 26th Regiment had practiced several amphibious assaults on San Clemente Island and the beaches at Camp Pendleton. On other occasions, they would assault the nearby practice beaches of Las Pulgas and Aliso, with hidden explosive discharges adding an additional degree of realism.

On July 12, 1944, a scheduled amphibious assault practice was cancelled, and the 26th Regiment was placed on alert status. All leave was cancelled and all personnel were advised to prepare to leave the United States. No information was provided about their target or what they were expected to do. The mood grew somber, especially among those Marines with wives and children back home.

All training was subsequently suspended, and the leave restrictions were also eased. Nationwide, families and other loved ones boarded trains and buses destined for San Diego, in hopes of having one last visit prior to the overseas deployment. George, Eddie, and Bob made one last trip up to Santa Monica. George said good-bye to his Aunt Lil, and Eddie exchanged addresses with his sweetheart next door.

As they returned to camp, all Marines pitched in to help pack their unit's equipment and prepare it for transfer overseas. The 26th Regiment was the only regiment leaving at the time. The men were instructed to store their nonessential personal items in a separate seabag, or box up the items to ship home. After the entire regiment had sorted through their belongings, a mountain of seabags was stacked in the barracks and stored in warehouses to await the 26th Regiment's eventual return.

On July 21st, all other personnel were ordered to prepare their combat packs. The rumors began to fly about when and where they would be deployed. The next morning, a convoy of trucks rumbled into the dusty streets of the 26th Regiment's wooden barracks and loaded both men and equipment. The convoy of trucks ambled their way past curious Southern California onlookers until they reached the Port of San Diego.

When they arrived at the docks, George boarded a troop-transport ship and found his assigned compartment. The hammocks were stacked six-high and gave little room for storing seabags or any other personal items. When George plopped down on his bunk, the man resting above him sagged only inches above his head.

Within minutes, George realized the poor air circulation below deck was going to make for a very long journey. Fortunately, he hadn't waited long before the overhead speaker bellowed out new orders allowing all Marines permission to roam the deck. They were not permitted to leave the fenced-in compound that was built around the dock and waterfront, but that didn't bother George. Anything was better than being cooped up below deck.

Four ships were needed to accommodate all elements of the 26th Regiment. After waiting almost two days for their equipment to be loaded, the Marines were relieved when Navy deckhands removed the mooring lines and made final preparations for their voyage. Once free of the docks, the lumbering ships glided past the port channel, through the submarine nets, and out to sea, escorted by several destroyers out on the horizon. As the ships slipped into the darkness, the city of San Diego seemed to disappear, since blackout conditions prevailed along the California coast.

With the ship accommodating hordes of sweaty men, the lower decks were steamy and reeked of body odor and diesel fuel. The odor and atmosphere were miserable on their own, but the steady rocking motion of the ship worsened conditions for those who already suffered from queasy stomachs. Many green-faced men could be found staggering their way above deck to steal some fresh air.

For most, this was their first experience on a Navy vessel. Corpsman Richard Overton of 2nd Battalion, "D" Company, realized the rocking ship was too much for his seasick stomach. He rushed to the deck looking for a place to vomit, and surprisingly found a clear spot. But as he hurried to the rail, other Marines standing nearby realized Overton's intentions and yelled "Stop!" Unfortunately, Overton learned by sad experience not to vomit upwind.[9]

Upon heading out to sea, the Marines aboard the transport ship heard an overhead announcement that the 26th Regiment was going to Hawaii. Later they would learn that the reason for their hasty departure was to assist in the invasion of Guam; at that time the 26th Marines were scheduled to be held in floating reserve for that operation.

Tension lifted when they understood that Hawaii was the destination, and the men began to relax by sunning themselves on the deck or reading novels provided by the Red Cross. Each unit gathered on the deck at a specific time for daily calisthenics and inspections. Six days into the voyage, they arrived at the port of Hilo, Hawaii, which would be their new home for the next six months, although the men did not know how long they would be stationed there.

CHAPTER FIVE

HAWAII IS HELL

Transporting the more than 3,300 men in the 26th Regiment was like moving a mountain. The logistical challenges of organizing meals, digging latrines, and transferring equipment from ship to shore required significant planning and organization.

Once all the Marines had disembarked, they marched into the town of Hilo, and were directed to a city park where they set up camp for the night. The "invasion" of Marines was surely a curiosity to the local population, especially for this once sleepy town that now played host to thousands of men in its public square.

Although the skies were clear, George and the remainder of his unit were instructed to find a companion and combine their shelter halves to erect a tent. A heavy rain was expected during the night. The intensity of a Hawaiian rainstorm took many by surprise, as they hadn't properly sealed their tents, and by morning, the waking Marines had to wring out their soaking wool blankets and pack their dripping shelter halves in their combat packs. It wasn't until mid-morning that the sun was hot enough to dry their soggy dungarees.[1]

By noon, the Marines had boarded narrow gauge railroad flatcars used to transport sugarcane. Disembarking the train cars, Marines watched as a convoy of trucks arrived, and soon George and his Fox Company Leathernecks were seated on rock hard benches in the back of a truck, feeling every bump, rock, and pothole on the unfinished dirt road. Their trek wound up the dusty roads through the saddle between Mauna Kea and Mauna Loa. After a half day long journey, they arrived at an abandoned tent city known as Camp Tarawa.

Camp Tarawa lay 2,600 feet above sea level, just outside the village of Kamuela, which was part of the Parker Ranch, the second largest cattle ranch on earth.[2] The camp was originally created in 1942 and was occupied by the Army in response to the threat of another Japanese invasion after Pearl Harbor was attacked. After a year and the battle of Midway, the threat to American soil diminished, and the camp was abandoned. A few months later, the battered 2nd Marine Division arrived in December 1943, and named the camp after the island they had just liberated. After the 2nd Marine Division left Hawaii to continue their "island-hopping" invasions, the camp sat idle until the newly created 5th Division arrived to take advantage of the ready-made training facility and make Camp Tarawa its home.

The camp was a sea of dusty, sagging old tents that was anything but encouraging to the bedraggled, travel weary Marines. But a massive clean-up detail quickly spruced up the encampment, and within days, Camp Tarawa was a functional military compound.

The camp was a perfect training location because of its unique topography. The Big Island of Hawaii has 13 different climate zones and is more

Camp Tarawa, Hawaii

than double the size of all the other Hawaiian Islands combined.³ Camp Tarawa sat in the middle of the two towering volcanoes Mauna Kea and Mauna Loa, and was only a twelve-mile hike from the coast. It also offered both tropical and desert climates that were helpful in mimicking all types of battle terrain.

Surrounding the camp, the rolling hills were mostly barren of vegetation, except for the abundant, nonnative cactus. Immigrants were thought to have imported the cactus seed in cattle feed that was brought to the island before the turn of the century. It was a hearty cactus impervious to the cool evenings, thriving in the daytime hot, dry air.

Just beyond the tent city was a patch of windblown trees that leaned away from the incessant breeze that tormented men with blowing airborne dust and dirt. The combination of dust and volcanic ash got in their eyes, irritated their lungs, and was a constant source of torment. PFC Glenn D. Chanslor of Fox Company, 2ⁿᵈ Battalion, 26ᵗʰ Regiment (2/26) remembered that the wind, dust and volcanic ash were so awful that taking a shower was almost pointless: "Just as you finished your shower, the gust of wind would sweep through the showers and you would be covered in the damn stuff from head to toe."

On the other side of Kamuela was the tropical zone, which boasted an extraordinary medley of native plants and animals. Among the countless varieties of lush trees and ferns, none were more spectacular than the native Ohia Lehua trees that would shimmer with silvery-green leaves and burst into bold red pompon flowers.⁴ All of these conditions made it possible to simulate any island environment that might be experienced in the coming months.

Aside from the administrative Quonset huts, the camp was comprised mostly of row after row of 16x16 foot tents. Each tent had a high, pointed roof, and the rows of tents resembled an assembly line of green pyramids. Each tent slept six men with enough space for a cot and a seabag.

George shared a tent with PFC Dean F. Keeley. Dean was tall —about six feet, four inches — and handsome with brown hair and a young face. George described Keeley as a likeable, overgrown kid. Keeley had attempted to join the Marines at 16, but the recruiter discovered his birth certificate had been altered and forced him to wait another year before enlisting.

Keeley wanted to be a Marine after seeing a MovieTone newsreel at a

Saturday matinee when he was 13. The newsreel reported on the Japanese-Chinese war, and Keeley remembered that a cameraman had secretly filmed a Japanese soldier torturing a Chinese mother. He remembered, "I vividly recall watching this Jap snatching a baby out of the Chinese mother's arms, and holding it by its feet, and smashing the baby's head against the wall. At 13 years old, you can't imagine the impression that made on me. But it was on this newsreel, this Japanese soldier, killing this baby, and then bayoneting the mother. Now, I watched that, and I couldn't believe it, but I couldn't forget it. It was indelibly etched in my mind."

Keeley remembered how much he loved his 10-year-old younger brother, and how determined he was to protect him from Japanese aggression. When Pearl Harbor was attacked, those feelings rekindled. Keeley stated, "I said to myself, those SOBs are never going to kill my brother... so I joined the Marines."[5]

With the 5th Division yet to be called into combat, Marine commanders took advantage of the extended training time. Despite victories at Tinian and Guam, important tactical lessons were learned during the conflicts in Saipan and Peleliu, and the newly developed combat strategies needed time to be properly implemented.

Because the Parker Ranch offered such a huge training area, massive battalion and even regimental-size training exercises were organized. George and his fellow Leathernecks endured drill after drill, field problem after field problem, and one amphibious assault after another. With few exceptions, everyone from George's unit found that the training at

Dean Keeley (right) posing with Glenn Russell, also of Fox Company

Camp Tarawa was more demanding and physically taxing than any training they had endured.

Fox Company survived many 12-mile forced marches down to the beach.
These grueling, no-rest-allowed marches pushed many Marines to exhaustion as they struggled with the heat and steep terrain.

George's platoon sergeant, Gunnery Sergeant Joseph Joyner, was a large
man, standing more than six feet tall and weighing over 200 pounds. His
reputation of yelling first and asking questions later ensured that most of
the men in the company didn't like him. Joyner was also known to use his
authority to goad Marines into making mistakes. As one forced march began, Joyner turned to George and taunted, "You're not going to make this
one, Doc!" George retorted "I'll be there when it hits the fan, don't you
worry about me."

The march was near its midpoint when Joyner began to fall behind the
company, struggling for breath and swaying from side to side. George slowed
his pace to get even with Joyner and asked, "Do you want me to take your
pack and rifle for you?" Joyner angrily quipped, "No damn corpsman's ever
going to take my pack and rifle," then quickened his pace. As they neared
the camp, the big man's stagger grew more pronounced, so George hailed
a jeep ambulance. Joyner collapsed and was taken back to camp where he
was treated and sent back to his tent. After that experience Joyner never
bothered George again. Platoon Sergeant Joseph Malone, a likeable leader
that everyone grew to respect, later replaced Sgt. Joyner.

By October of 1944, the men were getting antsy to either go into battle
or go back stateside. George had been in training with the Marines for ten
months, and he was wondering if he was ever going to see combat. As the
complaining intensified, the Marine brass responded by intensifying the
training. One-day field problems evolved into three-day field problems as
each unit would hike several miles up the mountains, organize their units
into skirmish lines, and practice attacking a make-believe enemy position.

One extended training exercise took them down to the beach, where
they practiced making amphibious landings and assaulting "Japanese" targets. George decided he wasn't going to shave because he was tired of the
morning ritual. Day after day, his beard and mustache grew longer and
more conspicuous. After the training exercise, which lasted about a week,
George looked in the mirror and saw a week's worth of caked on dust and

One of the training beaches near Camp Tarawa, Hawaii

dirt sticking to his beard and skin. It took an hour to clean off the grime, and in the end, George simply had to shave off the weeklong project, just to get clean. From that point on, George never wore a beard or mustache.

Increasingly frequent extended exercises put added pressure on corpsmen like George, who were not only required to treat the simulated wounds, but also the real injuries that inevitably occurred during long marches and mock battle simulations. The added training finally proved, to the once skeptical Marines, the importance and necessity of their Navy corpsmen. George, Eddie, Bob, and the other corpsmen were no longer "outsiders" from the Navy, but full-fledged Marines, and trusted members of the combat units. In return, the corpsmen developed a deep and enduring respect for the Marines who were eager to do their job at all costs.

Life at Camp Tarawa wasn't just all work and no play. The camp USO was a popular place to relax, especially when liberty time was limited.

The city of Hilo was the main liberty port, but getting there was difficult. The long route was to return the way they came, on the 60-mile dirt road through the "saddle" between Mauna Loa and Mauna Kea. The quick route was the coastal highway, which avoided the mountainous terrain and traversed the shoreline, but offered rocky cliffs and steep drop-offs. George made the trek to Hilo only once. He wasn't interested in carousing, and after seeing the limited activities available, he preferred to go to nearby Kamuela for his brief time on liberty.

George and Dean Keeley spent their free time camping "out in the boondocks" of the Parker Ranch, where they hunted rabbits and shot at targets. George grew up hunting with his father and younger brothers, and "taking to the hills" above Kamuela was the next best thing to being home.

Around Thanksgiving, rumors began to fly concerning a small wood-framed building that was built near division headquarters. Known as the "Conference Room," it re-

George and Eddie pose holding a captured Japanese flag while on liberty in Hawaii

quired a special pass to enter. All the windows were blackened and the doors had double locks. A tall, barbed wire fence was built around the building, and a gate leading into the encampment was heavily guarded around the clock.

Behind these closed doors, battle planners studied "Island X," and integrated battle and intelligence summaries from recent Pacific conflicts to organize the 5th Division's plan of attack. As strategies were formed, field-training tactics were modified to best implement the new plan. Division planners experimented with different combinations of infantry, artillery, and the integration of air and tank support, in hopes of finding the right combination for the "Island X" operation.

Training exercises reviewed basic combat tactics. Marines were repeatedly reminded to dig deeper foxholes, live-ammunition training intensified, and combat loading techniques on LST's were repeated time and again.

By December 1944, the 5th Division had been in training almost an entire year. With the buzz intensifying at Division and Regimental headquarters as new units arrived at camp—including an Army Amphibious Truck Unit that drove their DUKWs right into camp—it was evident that a trip to the battlefront was not far off.

Although D-day was approximately two months away, only a few division commanders knew the destination and timing of the upcoming conflict. Speculation was high that the island of Formosa (Taiwan) was the next likely target. *The Hawaii Advertiser*, a local newspaper, had managed to obtain and publish a strike photograph of bombs falling on Iwo Jima. The headline inquired "Is this the next target?"[6] Division intelligence officers were anxious after seeing the article, but because few had heard of the island, or knew of its strategic importance, it was dismissed as mere speculation.

On December 20 the beginning of a steady stream of equipment and supplies began to make the 60-mile trek down the mountain, where transport ships waited in the Port of Hilo. After a brief Christmas celebration, a convoy of trucks began operating around the clock.

All Marines attached to the 26th Regiment arrived at Hilo just after Christmas. They were assigned to the USS *Hocking*, (APA 121) which was waiting in port. George and his Fox Company Marines were assigned bunks four levels below deck. They each found their sleeping compartment—a hammock that rocked with the ship—and stowed their combat packs in the cramped space. George had the added burden of finding a place to store his medical kits, further limiting his movement. The mounting stockpile of supplies and equipment on the Hilo docks required the mobilization of Marines to help with the loading detail, and Dean Keeley was one Marine assigned to the task. While loading the ship, Keeley and his loading crew discovered an unopened box of Remmington .45 caliber pistols. Recognizing that these pistols were a prized possession reserved mostly for officers, Keeley and his crew secretly put the box aside and continued loading the ship. At the end of the day, they returned to open the box and found twelve pistols, each packaged in individual boxes. Keeley took two pistols and put them in his deep pockets; the other Marines quickly snatched up the rest.

With darkness looming, they were able to hide the pistols well enough to avoid detection as they boarded the ship for the night. They knew, however, that the missing pistols would cause an uproar. Sure enough an announcement overhead warned of the impending search for the missing weapons. Frantically trying to find a hiding spot, some hid their pistols by wedging them between the pipes above their bunks. Keeley thought that if he had some tape, he would hide his pistols in the large, horn-like air intakes up on the deck.

Quickly, he thought of George, who had rolls of tape in his medical bag. Nonchalantly, Dean whispered to George, "Do you have any tape I can borrow?"

Curious, George replied, "Why?"

Dean explained his predicament of having two stolen pistols.

George asked, "Do I get one?"

Dean agreed, and quickly George scrambled to retrieve some gauze and medical tape.

Both George and Dean enlisted the help of their friend Gaitano Arcuri, a slight 135-pound Marine who was willing to be their partner in crime. They held Arcuri by his legs and guided him down the shaft of the air intake. He tied gauze to the trigger guides and taped the gauze to the inside wall of the vent. Then they lifted him back to safety before quietly returning to their bunks, smothering laughter all the way down the gangways. After an exhaustive search, the officers couldn't find a single missing pistol. A week later when the commotion had died, Dean returned to the vent, pulled on the gauze and retrieved the pistols.

By January 4, 1945, the 5th Division had closed its operation at Camp Tarawa, and was aboard the *Hocking*, headed for Pearl Harbor to meet up with the other elements of the invasion force. Two days later, George stood on the deck of the *Hocking* and watched an armada of ships at Pearl Harbor. His crew still didn't know where they were going, but they were getting the impression it was going to be big.

Shore leave was granted in daily shifts. Marines spent much of their time getting their pictures taken with hula-girls, or hanging out in a host of tattoo shops, poolrooms or shooting galleries throughout Honolulu. The local YMCA and USO clubs were also packed with Marines, sailors, and soldiers.

After hearing that Honolulu was a stop-off on their journey, Captain Frank Caldwell learned his brother James was aboard a destroyer mine layer anchored at Pearl Harbor. James, seven years his senior, was assigned as the ship's gunnery officer and part of the invasion force headed for "Island X." Through a network of Marine chaplains, Caldwell made arrangements to visit his brother while he was on shore leave.

They met at a downtown Honolulu restaurant, and later went aboard his brother's ship and down into his spacious stateroom. There, he found maps and other charts scattered around the room. His brother asked, "Do you know where we're all going?"

Embarrassed that he was in command of 250 Marines, but was still in the dark about his destination, he shook his head no, and said, "They don't tell us those things."

James replied, "Do you want to know where you're going?"

Somewhat puzzled that a Naval officer—his brother—aboard a nondescript ship was privy to the secret that only a handful of Marine commanders knew, Frank replied, "How do you know?"

James stood and pointed to one of maps strewn around the room, and stated, "Here's the target, this little island of Iwo Jima." He then went into great detail, explaining the strategic significance of this seemingly useless piece of real estate. He stated that for many months, U.S. B-29s were making bombing runs over mainland Japan, but success was limited. For one reason, supplying bombs and other materials for the B-29s based in China was limited because their bases could only be resupplied by air. They were also hampered by the distance they had to fly to reach their targets. If they ran into any problems, they could run out of fuel before reaching the safety of the Chinese base.

In addition, B-29s based in the Marianas faced many challenges that the capture of Iwo Jima could resolve. The Japanese had installed sophisticated radar warning equipment on Iwo Jima, which provided their air defense network in Tokyo with a two-hour warning of an impending attack. Iwo Jima-based fighters were successful in harassing the attacking Superfortresses (B-29s), and to avoid them, B-29s expended critical fuel to go around the island.

B-29s were even more compromised by the severe Japanese winds that often hindered the bomber's airspeed over the target. Without fighter escort—and all of the current U.S. airfields were too far from the Japanese targets for fighters to accompany the bombers—the slower speeds simply made low-level bombing too costly in terms of both men and equipment. Consequently, bombers climbed to higher altitudes—usually 25,000 to 30,000 feet—and severely reduced their accuracy. [7]

The prospect of having an airstrip on Iwo Jima would allow P-51 Mustangs to be within range to escort the B-29s, their presence allowing an immediate improvement in both bombing accuracy and crew survivability. Quite simply, if the U.S. occupied Iwo Jima, Japan would face the same fate as Germany, which could not withstand the fierce and constant allied bombing.

Iwo Jima was also important in the psychological battle, as it was in Japan's "Inner Vital Defense Zone" and was considered Japanese soil. No foreign flag had ever flown on that land. Conquering Iwo Jima would deliver a stiff blow to Japanese confidence and morale.

Even though Captain Caldwell had discovered the secret of his combat destination, the 5th Division rank and file Marines still didn't know, but dutifully continued their final preparations for the invasion of "Island X." On January 4, the invasion force left Pearl Harbor, as Marine commanders had planned several amphibious landing rehearsals on Maui to further fine-tune their strategy.[8] Unfortunately, when the warm ocean air meets the cool air descending from the tall mountains on the island of Maui, the result is a constant, stiff wind. As the Marines attempted to land on Maui, the water was too choppy to do it safely, so the excursion was cancelled. The fleet of Higgins boats circled back to the transport ships, waiting their turn to load the Marines aboard their ship.

The constant rocking and pitching of the LCVP took its toll on Dean Keeley, who grew increasingly seasick. After an hour, he became so violently ill he couldn't stop vomiting. Even when there was nothing left in his stomach, he continued to heave. As Keeley recalled, "I got so seasick at first that I thought I was going to die, and then later I thought I wasn't going to die . . . or I wished I would die."

George could do nothing but simply stand by and watch Keeley suffer. After an hour circling the *Hocking*, George's first platoon took their turn to climb aboard. Keeley, too weak to stand, couldn't even contemplate climbing the rope nets to get aboard. The ship's crew was not authorized to use the hoist to retrieve a Marine unless a corpsman certified its use for safety reasons. George smiled, trying to keep a straight face at the sight of his friend lying in a helpless heap caused by, of all things, seasickness. George summoned the crew to engage the hoists and lower the net.

Keeley recalls "They dropped down a landing net, and put me in it, and drug me up by the hoist, and dropped my ass on the deck right there in front of George... and he never ever let me forget it!"

After a few more amphibious landings on other smaller Hawaiian islands, the convoy returned to Pearl Harbor to resupply and give the men one last shore leave. Days later, the entire invasion armada was organized just miles off the coast of Oahu and began its westward migration.

Finally, the invasion force was bound for its still unknown destination. Soon they would learn the real name of "Island X," and surely they would never forget it.

CHAPTER SIX

FINDING GOD

A s the distance grew between the 5th Division's convoy and Pearl Harbor, speculation was rampant concerning their target. On January 29, George and his Fox Company compatriots were ordered on deck for a briefing. 2nd Battalion Commander Lt. Colonel Joseph P. Sayers stood in front of the company with a serious demeanor. He held a long pointer in one hand, and with the other hand bent down to take hold of the corner of a white sheet. He cleared his throat and very dramatically announced, "Gentlemen, I am here to disclose that our target is. . ."A whooshing sound filled the air as he ripped the sheet off a large, brown relief map below. He paused between the words "Iwo —

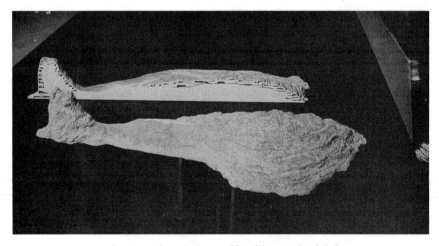

*A cross section relief map of Iwo Jima used to brief
Marines about the impending invasion*

Jima."[1] Having already learned about Iwo Jima from his brother, Captain Caldwell rolled his eyes upward and gave a quick exhale through his nose, in a half-laugh at Sayers' histrionics.[1]

Lt. Colonel Sayers spoke for several minutes, using his pointer as he described a few features on the rubber model relief map. The unit intelligence officers conducted the remainder of the briefing, pointing to a hill or other objective on the map. Fox Company listened to the latest reconnaissance and intelligence reports, based on information gathered over the past several months. Not only were they oriented to their unit's responsibility, they also learned the goals and objectives of each regiment and division. After the briefing, each man could take a turn at using stereographic glasses that gave a three-dimensional image of selected landmarks on the island.

These same briefings were occurring in wardrooms, galleys, and troop compartments throughout the ship, and on other ships in the convoy.

Knowing the target relieved some of the tension. It also helped to know that taking Iwo Jima was only expected to take a few days, a week or so at the most. At least that was the impression George was given by those who gave the briefing. He felt some relief from knowing the operation was going to be completed quickly, but apprehension about how he would react in combat began to fester in his mind and the monotonous ship's routine gave him plenty of time to think.

As the voyage continued, the tedious routine began to blur one day into the next. Just before dawn, general quarters were called because this was the most dangerous time each day for a submarine attack. During general quarters, seamen would scurry about, practicing getting to their battle stations.

The monotony was broken one day when general quarters was called during the day, and Sergeant Malone assigned a couple of Marines from Fox Company to go up on deck to man antiaircraft weapons. Upon hearing their orders, these two Marines headed up the galley-way and out of the troop compartment. The hatches clanged shut behind them and were fastened tightly. For the first time, George realized his vulnerability at being four levels below deck during general quarters. He felt smothered amid steel bulkheads, winding pipes and hundreds of sweaty Marines. The panic of helplessness was overwhelming, especially because he did not know if they were under a genuine attack. He was trapped, and he could do nothing about it.

When the "all clear" was sounded, George was determined never to be trapped again below deck, so he developed a plan for the next time. He tracked down Sergeant Malone and explained that the Marines going above deck for general quarters could be hurt if they were attacked. George offered to escort the men to the deck, just in case any of them were injured. Sergeant Malone considered George's reasoning, and then agreed. Subsequently, whenever general quarters was called, George followed closely behind the Marines and escaped the suffocating feeling of being trapped below deck.

After a week at sea, the odor of men, vomit, oil, and the stifling stale air had begun to take its toll on George and his fellow Marines. Being below deck was even more dreadful when these horrid smells were mixed with the wafting aroma of the day's meal. In fact, not everyone could bring himself to sleep below deck. Corpsman Dick Overton had such a strong aversion to the smells, and a fear of being trapped, that he slept on deck under a landing craft or a lifeboat. He wrapped himself in his wool blanket as he settled on the hard deck to sleep on top of his shelter half. When it rained, he got wet, but he remained warm wrapped in his blanket. The only night he didn't sleep on the deck was the night before D-day.[2]

During the long, tedious days, men found amusing ways to keep themselves occupied. Aside from the routine calisthenics and weapons inspections, Marines were treated to band concerts or an occasional amateur show. To break the monotony, several men, including Corpsman Bob Ray, decided to fashion rings out of silver dollars. They banged, hammered, and filed the coins for days until each had created a recognizable ring bearing unique designs.

Mess call was another time killer. Men would stand in line for over an hour waiting for the mess to open. Each table could serve six to eight men. While they ate standing, coffeepots hung from hooks attached to an overhead cable, allowing the pots to sway with the ship. In rough waters, it helped to have a buddy who could hold on to your coffee mug while you poured.

At times, the ocean was so calm that the convoy of ships appeared to be floating in a gigantic mirror. Marines spent hours on deck leaning with both arms on the rail hoping to see a change in the scenery.

On good days, flying fish were spotted in the distance while porpoises frolicked carelessly in the ship's wake, providing precious entertainment for the mind-numbed Marines.

"Aboard on deck the USS Hocking at dusk. Marines line the rail watching the receding sun. Perhaps no words are spoken as the men stare off into the distance, each having their own thoughts on what the next few days may bring. Or perhaps they are watching flying fish jump from the water and race the ship. Whatever though, once the sun sets there is a long period of quiet deep thought afterward as each man leaves the railing."
(By Richard E. Overton, Corpsman D/2/26 on Iwo Jima. Pencil on paper.)

On February 5, word filtered down to the Marines below deck that land was spotted off in the distance. George, Eddie, and a handful of other Fox Company Marines scrambled up the gangways and wormed their way topside. As they reached the railing, they could see the small atoll of Eniwetok off in the distance.[3] The inlet to the lagoon was protected by submarine nets, and each ship navigated past the buoys, free from the threat of enemy attack. [4]

George jostled for his position at the railing as Marines streamed topside to watch the *Hocking* enter the huge lagoon. The wreckage of ships and other vehicles still cluttered the beaches, evidence of the 4th Division's recent battle to wrest the island from the Japanese. From the lagoon, the island looked like a large turtle floating in the midst of the huge ocean, but stripped and blackened palm trees and vegetation had yet to recover from the recent shelling. The ship dropped anchor, and within minutes the shipboard communication system bellowed a message, "Now hear this… now hear this… all nonessential personnel are permitted to go overboard to swim." A collective cheer rang through the ship as men peeled off their dungarees and flung them to the deck. Men hurled themselves overboard and splashed in the refreshing cobalt blue water like preschoolers in a kiddy pool.[5] The anxiety of the upcoming invasion and the constant threat of submarine attacks were suddenly lifted as Marines had finally escaped the cooped up quarters that confined them.

Only a few senior officers and their staff went ashore for last-minute intelligence briefings and planning meetings. Each ship in the convoy took a turn to refuel, and after two days, the entire convoy assembled outside the lagoon and resumed their westward migration.

By February 11, they had reached Saipan, and Marines prepared for their final amphibious rehearsed landing. After the anchor was set, troops were ordered to immediately prepare for debarkation and assault of the island of Tinian, which could be seen several miles away.

Just as they had rehearsed countless times before, they lined up in their troop compartment in full gear and waited for the signal to proceed. At the signal, they walked through the gangways and tried to avoid banging their helmets, combat packs, and rifles on bulkheads and overhangs as they made their way on deck. Once on deck, they quickly found their preassigned debarkation stations, and stood by as each man took his turn climbing down the rope nets onto the landing craft.

The sea was perilously rough, and some men were nearly crushed by the troopship and LCVP colliding in the choppy water. When the wind intensified, planners cancelled the intended landing, and the Higgins boats were ordered back to their mother ships. But with the staggering number of similar-looking troopships bobbing about in the unprotected bay (there were over 800 ships in the convoy), the crews of many LCVPs became disoriented. The Marines of Dog Company of the 2/26 spent over four hours bobbing in the whitecapped ocean in their landing craft and baking in the hot sun until finally locating the *Hocking*.[6]

By February 16, portions of the invasion force had already left Saipan. Some ships were sent days earlier to participate in the preinvasion bombing of Iwo Jima. During the early morning hours, the *Hocking* and the remainder of the 4th and 5th Division convoy had quietly left Saipan's harbor. D-day was a little more than 72 hours away.

The routine of calisthenics, inspections, and debarkation drills continued, not only to sharpen the skills and preparation of each Marine, but also to lessen the anxiety that became more palpable with each passing hour.

Lying on his bunk, George pondered his situation, growing increasingly worried about how he would respond in the heat of battle. He thought of his closest friends like Eddie Monjaras, Bob Ray, Bob DeGeus, and Dean Keeley. He was surrounded by good, admirable young men he had grown to love as brothers. Throughout the past year, they had covered for each other's mistakes, slept in the rain together, shared foxholes, and ate mountains of Spam. They had come to know each other's innermost aspirations, irritating habits, and idiosyncrasies. With only hours left before D-day, George faced the real prospect of being killed or, worse yet, watching his friends being killed.

Fear began to consume George, but it was not the fear of death. Dying was not a great concern. Above all, George worried that he would be incompetent—either from fear or dereliction of duty—and would cause one of his friends to be killed.

Marines were trained to find protection behind a rock or in a shell hole if they were wounded. They knew they must immediately get out of the line of fire. Conversely, corpsmen were trained to go out into the line of fire and retrieve, protect, and treat the wounded.

Although George had been trained to treat fractures, apply tourniquets, and attend to shrapnel wounds, he was also trained to recognize combat fatigue. He saw some of those symptoms in himself, and it bothered him knowing that he could end up as one of those walking wounded. He couldn't stop agonizing over whether he could perform his duty when a friend's life depended on it. For the first time in his life, George realized his humbling situation.

Although George was raised among Mormons in Northern Utah, he didn't attend church services, and he tried to avoid religious activities whenever he could. After joining the military, he occasionally attended church services, but mostly to avoid a duty more difficult than listening to a sermon. Today, the circumstances were different. He wanted to believe in a God, and if he was ever going to get help from God, there was no better time to ask for His help than now.

As he rested on his hammock, his hands behind his head, he closed his eyes and hoped nobody was watching him. He hesitated, not knowing what to say, but for the first time in his life, he quietly whispered a prayer. He asked God to help him do his job, regardless of the circumstances he faced. But he couldn't bring himself to ask for protection from being killed. Disgrace was worse than death. He shared that belief with most Marines, who cared more about living without shame than being killed.

Soon after he ended his short prayer, a calm, serene feeling came over him. He had never felt like this before, and he couldn't ignore the peacefulness that enveloped him. Just as he nodded off to sleep, he was strangely confident that a God existed after all.

CHAPTER SEVEN

"OPERATION DETACHMENT"

"I don't know who he is, but the Japanese General running this show is one smart bastard."

— *Lt. General Holland M. Smith, Commander,*
Fleet Marine Force Pacific

The months of planning, training, and preparation were finally concluding, as "Operation Detachment" was only hours away from implementation.

Lieutenant General Tadamichi Kuribayashi of the Imperial Japanese Army likewise was making his final preparations for the invasion he knew was about to begin. Japanese intelligence had notified Kuribayashi of the departure of the American armada from Saipan just four days earlier. The warning had given him ample time to deploy his forces into their fighting stations.[1]

General Kuribayashi was a solemn, stone-faced officer, even by

Lieutenant General Tadamichi Kuribayashi

Japanese standards. Ironically, his contemporaries bemoaned his lack of humor. He had studied in Canada and the United States in the late 1920's, and had developed an understanding of American battle tactics. When he returned to Japan, he earned increased responsibility commanding cavalry units in Manchuria and China. His outstanding military reputation, accompanied by his aristocratic upbringing, made him one of only a few Japanese soldiers ever granted an audience with Emperor Hirohito. He was later handpicked by Japanese Premier General Hideki Tojo to defend Iwo Jima.

Kuribayashi was devoutly loyal to the homeland and the Emperor, but was painfully realistic about the prospect of successfully defending Iwo Jima. He contradicted his superiors by warning that building airstrips on Iwo Jima could ultimately backfire because they held little strategic value. If the island were to fall into American control, the airstrips—and the island's relative closeness to the mainland—could become a real threat to Japanese security. However, his warnings went unheeded.

Kuribayashi considered two primary strategies for defending Iwo Jima. One option was to find a way to destroy the island, thus reducing its strategic usefulness to the Americans. The other option was to exact such a high price from the enemy that they would second-guess future attacks. The first option was simply unrealistic so he opted for the latter. In June 1944, his preparations began in earnest.

The island was a miserable place that reeked of rotting eggs from sulfur pots, and was infested with flies and other annoying insects. Because of the high sulfur content, the natural water was not potable, and Kuribayashi relied on rainwater to supply his troops. In a letter to his wife, Kuribayashi wrote of the critical lack of water:

> "Our sole source of supply is rainwater. I have a cup of water to wash my face—actually, my eyes only, then Lieutenant Fujita [his aide] uses the water. After he is through with it, I keep it for toilet purposes. The soldiers, in general, don't even have that much. Every day, after I've inspected defense positions, I dream in vain of drinking a cup of cool water. There are a lot of flies. Also many cockroaches crawl all over us. They are very dirty. Fortunately, there are no snakes or poisonous reptiles."[2]

U.S. intelligence had identified construction on the island, and bombing occurred sporadically. Significant attacks intensified as bombing was used as a diversionary measure during the invasion of Saipan in June 1944. Bombing continued throughout the summer and fall of 1944, but it had little effect on the operation of the two airstrips. As the year progressed, the incessant and unrelenting bombing attacks eventually galvanized Kuribayashi's determination to build a network of defenses under the surface of Iwo Jima.

His strategy was threefold. First, he constructed an amazing labyrinth of tunnels, spanning over 15 miles, connecting over 1,500 reinforced concrete pillboxes, observation points, and coastal defenses. (U.S. intelligence failed to recognize this vital element of the Japanese defense strategy until it was almost too late.) Second, Kuribayashi planned for the total destruction of his troops. No man, not even Kuribayashi, had any hope of leaving the island alive. Third, Japanese soldiers were instructed to kill at least ten Americans before they themselves perished. If the plan was to succeed, the 21,000 Japanese troops would exact over 250,000 American lives. At the beginning of the invasion, it appeared as though his plan would succeed. In retrospect, Kuribayashi's unique strategy for defending Iwo Jima remains among the most ambitious in the history of warfare.

In contrast, Marine General Harry Schmidt had a plan of assaulting Iwo Jima that was simple and straightforward. The top command for the Americans was Admiral Raymond A. Spruance of the Fifth Fleet and Vice Admiral Richmond Kelly Turner, who oversaw the Joint Expeditionary Forces. Under Spruance and Turner was Lt. General Holland M. Smith, who directed the Marine's expeditionary forces. Although Smith was a subordinate, he was a high profile general who often ruffled the feathers of his superiors.

Schmidt issued his operation plan in late December 1944; the first priority of the attack was to wrest Mount Suribachi from the Japanese and eliminate their main tactical vantage point. Upon securing the high ground, both the 4th and 5th Divisions would join forces, shoulder to shoulder, and continue their sweep northwest across the island, with the 3rd Division held in floating reserve.

The assault plan also called for ten days of preinvasion bombardment. The Navy complained that it didn't have enough ammunition or time to bomb for ten days so it counterproposed having three days only. Despite the pleadings of Marine brass, the Navy stuck to its three-day commitment. Weather delays and poor reconnaissance diminished the three days to fewer than 15 total hours of bombing actually being accomplished, a fact that translated into a much higher casualty rate among the infantry.[3]

The Americans had assembled an invasion force unlike anything seen in the Pacific theater. The huge strike force consisted of more than 70,000 troops and required 880 ships to transport and support them. These Marines were battle tested, well trained, and better armed than any invasion force yet to be organized. It was the largest Marine force ever assembled for a single invasion. On paper, Iwo Jima should have fallen in a matter of days. General Schmidt even predicted that Iwo Jima would fall within ten days. He later regretted making this prediction.

The first blow in the invasion was struck on February 16, but not at Iwo Jima. Admiral Spruance had dispatched a surprise attack from a carrier strike force (58) on Tokyo and the Nagoya-Kobe region, and destroyed hundreds of Japanese aircraft. The effect of the attack was not just one of destroying military targets. It shocked an already frightened Japanese citizenry and redirected their focus on homeland matters. This carrier task force, commanded by Admiral Marc Mitscher, then steamed back to Iwo Jima to engage in the preinvasion bombardment.

Two days prior to the invasion (D-2), Navy and Marine underwater demolition teams (UDT) approached the eastern beaches of Iwo Jima, escorted by LCI-R's (Landing Craft Infantry-Rockets) with guns and rockets ablaze. At this point, General Kuribayashi made his only tactical blunder of the campaign by assuming that this UDT attack was the main invasion, and he authorized the highly concealed coastal batteries to open fire. When the Japanese revealed these previously unknown coastal batteries, Navy vessels came to the rescue to blast them with their large guns. Although the damage was minimal to the Japanese defenses, the Navy learned of hundreds of new targets. As a result, significant changes were made to the invasion plan that likely saved countless Marines.

On the evening of D-1, a gloomy group of Marine commanders had read and reread the latest intelligence reports and were unable to mask their dejection. At a press briefing held by Marine generals and Navy brass, the somber tone was set by General Holland M. "Howlin' Mad" Smith, who predicted as many as 15,000 casualties. But after the dire predictions, Secretary of the

General Holland M. "Howlin' Mad " Smith

Navy James Forrestal stood to speak, saying, "Iwo Jima…leaves very little choice except to take it by force of arms, by character and courage."[4]

H-hour was set for 0900, and nothing could be done except to proceed as planned. Just before 0200, most of the Marines from the 4th and 5th Divisions were awakened and began their preparations for the beach assault. Only the troops assigned to the transport ships USS *Darke*, *Deuel*, and George's *Hocking* were excluded from the initial attack; they remained in division reserve.

Floating several miles off the coast of Iwo Jima was the flotilla of 43 troop transport ships, simultaneously serving some 50,000 meals of steak and eggs to the anxious Marines. In a well-coordinated logistical scheme, the now well fed Leathernecks simultaneously prepared to disembark their troopship and board their waiting landing craft.

While the crews of both divisions' ships were making final preparations before loading, the *Hocking* remained quiet. Filled with anxiety and apprehension, few men, including George, were able to sleep. George remained in his bunk, dressed in his fatigues and "boondockers," ready to don his combat pack at a moment's notice. Half asleep, he dozed only briefly, unaware that the invasion had already begun.

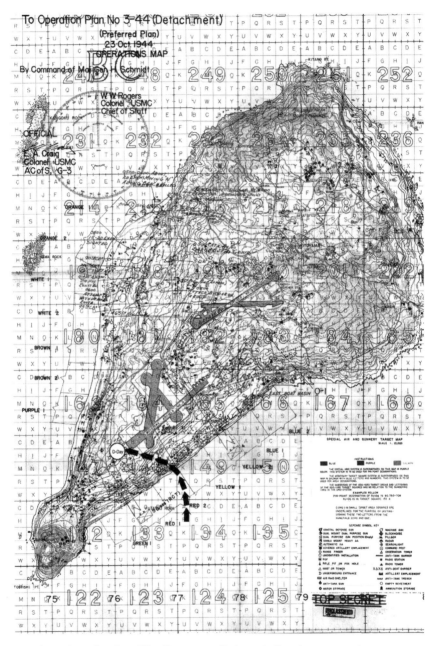

Approximate location of Fox Company on D-day as indicated on an operations map

"Iwo Jima is the most heavily fortified and capably defended island in the world. It will be a tough fight."
— *Vice Admiral Richmond K. Turner, Commander,*
Task Force 51

G eorge was suddenly roused at 0300 to the sound of an ear-piercing whistle over the ship's speaker system. When it stopped seconds later, an uncommon stillness hung throughout the holds below deck. George rested his weight on his elbows as he lifted his head as high as he could without bumping into the hammock above him. He listened intently to identify why it was so quiet, and after rubbing his eyes, he realized that the ship's ever present rumble had changed from its typical drone to a low pitched hum. After a few seconds, he could sense the ship was hardly moving, a strange feeling after weeks of being at sea.

George opted to get out of bed, rather than lie there for a few minutes more. He was too anxious to think about food, but when the mess call sounded overhead several minutes later, he wanted to use the opportunity to think of something other than the invasion. He ambled down the gangway to see what was being served for breakfast. To George's surprise, the mess kitchen produced a tempting odor that smelled strangely appealing. When he finally made it to the counter, Navy cooks were scooping out the last of steak and eggs, a typical battle-day fare. George felt fortunate to have a tray full of real—not powdered—eggs, and a small, but deliciously dry steak.

The *Hocking* was like most troop transport ships, offering enlisted men no chairs on the mess deck, but a waist-high table and a place to stand. While George stood at the table, shoulder to shoulder with a group of Marines eating their meals, he tried to savor the taste of the steak, but he couldn't keep his mind from racing. His train of thought was interrupted as the ship's loudspeakers began broadcasting the radio transmissions between Marine and Navy commanders in the final stages of the initial assault.[1] Reports of battle damage to gun emplacements and other targets gave the impression that the island was being obliterated. George thought to himself, surely nothing could survive such a pounding.

George finished his meal and walked slowly to the weather deck to watch the invasion unfold. At approximately 0800, an hour and a half of naval shelling was just concluding, and George watched as carrier-based fighters began to strike selected targets near the beach and on the slopes of the most dominant feature on the island, Mount Suribachi.[2]

As George watched the fighter planes finish their bombing runs, high altitude B-24 heavy bombers began to pound the island's surface, causing huge explosions. But some bombs missed the island and landed in the ocean, creating towering geysers in the salty water.[3] The Navy ships resumed their bombing at approximately 0830. Just minutes before H-hour at 0900, the commander of the 28th Marines requested that the Navy cease bombing operations in preparation for their initial landing.[4]

At the hour of attack, or "H-hour," George stood on the deck of the *Hocking* and strained to hear the drone of voices over the public-address system. Offshore spotters described how easily the first seven battalions had landed ashore, and their initial reports suggested that the resistance was light. As the hordes of Marines initially progressed inland, an officer reported that the first few minutes of the invasion were going "so far, so good." [5] Conditions didn't stay that way.

At H-hour +1, or 1000 hours, Marine casualties began to escalate rapidly as the enemy intensified attacks onshore. Japanese artillery and mortar positions had pre-sited their weapons for the entire southern landing area. Just when the beaches were most cluttered with men and equipment, the Japanese let fly a barrage of heavy weapons on the helpless Marines precariously waiting to get ashore.[6] Some landing vehicles took a direct hit, and men screamed in agony as they were left trapped and burning inside.

Others leaped from the flames into the water, only to be met with exploding artillery shells. Within minutes, the beaches were strewn with burning and disabled amtracs (amphibious tractors), DUKWs, and other landing craft.[7] Through the chaos, the well-trained Marines scrambled ashore and fanned out on the beach. Despite the intense offensive, the second and third waves of Marines continued to stream ashore.[8]

For Marines who landed in subsequent waves, the barrage of mortar fire caused confusion between line officers and their men.[9] Despite attempts to organize the men into skirmish lines, the plan was further delayed when the intense noise and an inability to mobilize radio equipment hampered communication.

Another significant obstacle came in the form of Iwo Jima's unforgiving black volcanic sand. Many compared it to trying to walk on coffee grounds. Each step took effort, and within minutes, the exhausted Marines were slowed to a crawl. Even the amtracs struggled to get traction in the ashy sand.[10]

Fifth Division Marines take momentary cover in a huge shell crater while awaiting the signal to renew D-day attack on the Iwo Jima island fortress

The Marines fought on, and advanced only 300 yards onto firmer ground, but Japanese mortarmen—positioned perfectly from their vantage points on Mount Suribachi—began their deluge of deadly mortars and artillery shells upon the hordes of pinned down Marines. Each booming mortar burst brought danger, as the hot metal ripped limbs and body parts from the helpless Marines. Shrapnel swooshed in every direction, severing anything soft within its trajectory. Corpsmen scrambled to treat the multiplying number of gruesome wounds that seemed to occur with every blast. With no place to hide, men frantically began to dig holes in the soft soil, desperate to find some cover from the mortar shells raining from the sky; but with each stroke of their shovel-like entrenching tools, the soft sand would dribble back in to refill the holes.

A disaster was in the making. Marines ashore were pinned down by a hailstorm of artillery and mortar shells. The beaches were choked with disabled and burning equipment, and reinforcements could find no opening to get ashore. General Kuribayashi, the brilliant Japanese commander over the 21,000 Japanese forces on Iwo Jima, had planned to allow the Americans to get onto shore, but be unable to retreat. Once on shore, he planned to cut off their advance and annihilate the Americans as they were stranded on the beach.[11] By doing so, he hoped to avoid being overwhelmed by the American's superior numbers. At 1030 hours, Kuribayashi's plan was working.

Meanwhile, the combat play-by-play continued to blare on the *Hocking*'s public address system. George and many of the men from 2/26 having made their way topside after breakfast, stood anxiously watching the action, leaning over the railing to view the battle from their safe distance several miles off shore.[12] Watching from such a distance gave George some sense of what was happening on shore. With each explosion came a brilliant white flash of light, and a plume of dust and smoke. The detonation was heard a few seconds later. Seeing the far-off explosions, and lacking any clear view of the beach, they relied on the conversations from the ship's overhead speakers, and they trusted the rosy assessment of the battle during those first few hours. Some men grew frustrated that they were still stuck onboard and weren't part of the rout they assumed was occurring. Some openly complained that all the good souvenirs would be taken. They could do nothing but wait their turn to go ashore.

Marines await their turn as they watch from a safe distance offshore...
Dozens of types of ships comprised the Iwo Jima invasion armada

Back on the beach, the horror of men being shot or being hit by exploding shell fragments caused confusion among many Marines. Commanders screamed at the indecisive troops to get off the beach. Veteran Marines led by example and charged forward amidst the exploding shells and bullets. Officers called in naval guns to blast the exposed artillery positions that were inflicting heavy casualties on the advancing troops. Carrier-based planes— "Corsairs" (F-4U's) and "Hellcats" (F-6F's)—bombed and strafed hidden emplacements on the slopes of Mount Suribachi.[13]

Aboard LSTs (landing ship, tank), troops attempting to land tanks onto the beach had endured failure after failure. Many were taken out by the steep beaches, soft sand, or disabling mines; but by 1130, Sherman tanks were rumbling across the terrace above the sandy beach, directly engaging the enemy gun positions and taking some of the pressure off the Marines on foot.[14]

Shortly after 1130 hours, the 26th Marine Regiment were ordered to begin their debarkation.[15] The whistle from the *Hocking*'s bo'sun blared overhead ordering all Marines to report to their troop compartment and prepare to disembark. The ship was abuzz with activity, as men hurried here and there to get ready for this well rehearsed debarkation.

George grew even more anxious as he wrestled with two competing emotions. On one hand, he was ecstatic about getting off the foul-smelling dungeon of a ship that had been his home for the past seven weeks. But self-doubt still gnawed at his stomach, and he feared he might be a coward in the face of battle. The last thing he wanted to do was to disappoint the Marine cohorts that he had grown to love and respect. Having little time to dwell on these feelings, he quickly stepped down the maze of ladders and squeezed through hatches as swarms of other Marines also made their way to their assigned positions below deck. They had been through this drill a hundred times, and in the cramped space, they helped each other don combat packs, helmets, and weapons awaiting the next whistle. George stood anxiously tightening straps and adjusting his entrenching tool to prevent it from poking the man who followed behind him.

After a seemingly interminable ten-minute wait, the whistle pierced the low rumble of muted voices engaging in nervous small talk. George made one last check of his bunk to ensure that he had left nothing behind. As each man stepped up to clear the narrow hatchways, helmets and rifles clanged against steel as gear inadvertently banged against the narrow openings. Up on the weather deck, each man found his assigned debarkation spot and inched his way to the rail, where the rope nets had already been lowered over the edge of the ship.

The wind whipped through the ship's railing and whitecaps splashed over the rolling swells. Bouncing below the rope, the LCVP sputtered in the water, waiting for its cargo of Leathernecks to board. Each man carefully balanced his weight as he lifted a leg over the rail and cautiously stepped onto the netting. This tricky descent had been practiced repeatedly in both calm and choppy waters. Each man concentrated on each downward step, taking great care not to crush the hands of the man below. The surging surf made the LCVP lunge high on the rolling waves and descend rapidly below the *Hocking*'s water line. Most men properly timed their release from the rope and landed safely on the deck of the landing craft. A handful of others guessed poorly and landed hard on the deck, just as the boat was at its farthest distance at the bottom of a swell. Fewer men, still, let go of the netting just as the boat reached its apex, lost their balance and collapsed hard on the bulwark of the LCVP.

George, near the end of the line, made it safely aboard the LCVP without incident. Having watched several Marines muddle their way aboard, he was careful not to make mistakes.

When the "away all boats" order sounded over the public-address system, George stood shoulder to shoulder with his platoon-mates in the Higgins boat as the engine growled to life. The sudden lurch caused each man to take a quick step backward to readjust his stance. George, near the back of the boat, watched as helmets swayed and men jumped in unison with the bouncing vessel. The flotilla of landing craft cleared their respective troopships and began to shape their attack formation.

Watching the bombardment of Mount Suribachi, a Higgins boat crewmember
prepares to come ashore on D-day

The starting line: signalman on standby to give "the word"

Aboard their Higgins boat, George and his platoon were stuck in a circling pattern with the other LCVPs of the regiment. George peered over the wall of the boat, watching the orange and yellow flashes on Mount Suribachi, not knowing that the cluttered beaches were the reason for their delayed landing.

The flotilla of landing craft circled several miles offshore, waiting for the anticipated signal, but the wreckage and debris continued to mount.[16]

George was growing weary of sputtering about offshore, waiting for the signal to go ashore. During the several hours of waiting, Marines onshore assigned to clear the debris were working feverishly, despite the ongoing shelling, to clear the shores.

By late afternoon, the word finally came for the 26th Marines to come ashore. Adrenaline surged through George's veins, and he held on tight to his combat pack as the boat lunged through the waves. Within minutes, Mount Suribachi to his left had begun to dominate his view. But at eye level, the landscape was filled with wreckage and destroyed vehicles and landing craft.

Anxious Marines await their landing on D-day

George stood on his toes, watching the warplanes attack the steep slopes of Suribachi. One by one, fighter planes would peel off from their formation and dive menacingly toward the cone-shaped mountain. The bombs released from the belly of each plane exploded in a bright yellow ball of flame, and the pilot would quickly veer to avoid collision with the mountain.

From the vantage point of the landing craft, Marines next to George commented on the performance of each fighter pilot's dive near the surface of the mountain before dropping his payload. For the more daring pilots who chose to fly closest to the mountain, Marines would yell "Single." For pilots not quite as adventurous, the Marines would yell out disappointingly "Married."[17] George could only muster a nervous smile at the sarcastic comments.

Several hundred yards from the beach, LCVPs idled side by side in the choppy water, waiting for the go-ahead to land. Seeing the path of the waiting invasion boats, Japanese mortarmen traversed their weapons and launched a practice round directly in the path of the oncoming American landing craft.

As the Higgins boats sputtered in formation, George thought to himself, "We're sitting ducks out here...let's get out of here." Finally, the wave commander cupped his hands around his mouth and shouted, "Go...Go...Go!" The coxswain yanked on the throttle, and the engines roared to life. Suddenly the line of LCVPs cut through the white-tipped waves and aimed for the assigned landing spot, Red Beach #2.

The skilled Japanese mortar teams knew just when to drop their mortar shells in the mortar tube, calculating the precise moment when the Americans would collide with the shells. George watched helplessly as one LCVP took a direct hit, jumping away from its path, and propelling helmets, Garand rifles and Marines through the air.

George and his platoon-mates watched in stunned silence as the events unfolded. Suddenly an exploding shell landed in the water just yards in front of them, and the plume of water drenched many men within. Realizing the risks of keeping their heads up, they all hunkered down to protect themselves from the barrage.

Mortar teams renew their attack on the Iwo Jima island fortress

When the LCVP hit the beach, the boat's ramp was unhooked from inside, and the nearest Marines leaned their shoulders into it several times to free it from its latches.

Slowly the LCVP opened its jaw-like door, splashing down in the waist-high surf. The Marines poured out on the beach, fanning out behind the terrace to avoid the lethal accuracy of Japanese machine gunfire coming from every direction.

Once the troops had spread out on the beach, Japanese gunners trained their weapons on the larger concentrations of Marines still struggling to come ashore. Dead Marines were scattered everywhere throughout the beach. Some lay face down in the sand; others were missing limbs in pools of fresh blood.

In survival mode, George ignored the dead Marines and scrambled up the beach. He crouched next to a junior officer, wanting to be sure he didn't miss the next command to find safer ground inland.

Chapter Nine

D-day Afternoon

On the beach, George and his unit waited for instructions to move further inland. Huddled next to his platoon leader, he fleetingly gripped at the sand that only slid through his fingers as he searched unsuccessfully for something substantial to hide behind.

The noise was intense and terrifying, and the impact of exploding shells rattled his bones and seemed to twist his internal organs. The clamor of vehicles, whooshing projectiles, and the barrage of explosions created a cacophony of sounds that further confused George and the men of his unit.

Marine Corps amtracs and medium tanks, blasted by Japanese artillery after they bogged down in the soft black volcanic ash of Iwo Jima, litter the beach as other Marines examine the wreckage

Onshore, the landing parties were still taking heavy casualties from mortar fire from Suribachi and other places yet to be discovered. A lucky few found refuge in large craters made by 16-inch shells from the ships offshore. These holes provided protection from horizontal gunfire, but offered little or no protection from the enemy's high-angle fire.

PFC Rudolph "Rudy" Mueller was in the 3rd platoon of Fox Company, and his unit had finally advanced past the second and third terraces. Mueller saw a Marine lying prone, aiming his rifle, and he appeared to have a good vantage point on the enemy's position. Mueller dashed toward the Marine, wanting to help him eliminate the gun emplacement that was halting their progress. As Mueller landed in the soft sand, he noticed that the Marine was not moving, and on closer inspection, saw a bullet hole through his helmet. The man had died instantly. Mueller thought, "This man still had breakfast in his stomach, and there he's dead already."

Eager to get off the beach, George's unit waited for instructions to move out, but confusion and chaos on the beaches limited communication between units. Despite the intensified bombardment of the beach, George watched as Marine artillery regiments endeavored to get ashore.

His unit was pinned down for over an hour until other advancing units neutralized much of the resistance from machine gun emplacements. When

Dead Marine lying on a slope of a shell crater still clutching his bayonet

the order came to move, George grabbed his carbine and medical bag and blended in with the other Marines who were forming a skirmish line. They began their advance inland toward Motoyama Airfield #1.

Like every corpsman in the Pacific, George was not issued a Red Cross armband to identify him as a corpsman. The lessons learned from the island hopping campaigns of the previous two years had taught the Americans that, unlike the Germans, the Japanese considered corpsmen important targets, similar to officers and NCOs. George was trained to blend in with the other Marines, and not lag behind his platoon. It was important to George that he not be separated from his unit. He feared being assigned to a group of nameless Marines that he didn't know, or who didn't care about him.

By 1700, much of the inland area beyond the beach had been secured. The 26th Marines advanced toward the southern end of Motoyama Airfield #1 and prepared to button-down for the night. PFC Glenn Chanslor recalls approaching a slope toward the airfield where a group of Marines stood, rifles slung over their shoulders, discussing a deceased Marine draped with a poncho.

Glenn asked, "What's going on?"

A solemn faced Marine replied dutifully as he looked down at the corpse, "That's John Basilone." The word of his death was whispered from one Marine to the other, who respectfully walked past the body.

"Manila John" Basilone, from Raritan, New Jersey, was a legendary Medal of Honor recipient from the battle at Guadalcanal. He was a reluctant hero who refused to be exiled to a noncombat assignment on the war-bond circuit. He was featured in *Life* magazine, and was adored by movie stars and dignitaries. Despite his celebrity status, he refused to be "a museum piece" and asked to return with his men.[1]

He was attached to 2/27, and many times during the long months of training at Camp Tarawa, Basilone was called on to give pep talks to the battle-hungry Marines who were struggling to stay focused. He was well liked and respected by everyone. He died in an attempt to single-handedly eliminate a gun emplacement up the slopes toward the runway of Airfield #1. He took a direct hit from a mortar shell and died along with four others. His last words were "Come on, you guys, let's get these guns off the beach."[2]

Captain Caldwell's Fox Company was ordered to build a perimeter defense at the base of the airfield, where the regimental headquarters had been set

Gunnery Sergeant "Manila John" Basilone

up. Within the perimeter was the fire direction center of the artillery regiment for the 5th Marine Division, and all were targets of Japanese artillery and mortar fire.

At 1800, the din of exploding shells and machine gunfire grew more intense, as newly arrived Marine artillery units were positioned inland toward Mount Suribachi. By 1830, these big guns began their assault on pillboxes and concrete bunkers that still remained unscathed by the day's bombardment. But there was little daylight left.

Within minutes after sunset, the hazy, smoke-filled sky was enveloped in darkness, and a new, more frightening war unfolded.

Facing the outline of Mount Suribachi, George began digging his rifle pit. With each stroke of his entrenching tool, he could feel the steam rise from the moist soil. The regulation foxhole, or "rifle pit," as the Marines called it, was six feet long, three feet deep, and four feet wide. It was designed for two men, one to take his turn on watch while the other slept. With an odd number of Marines in his platoon, though, George was left by himself in his foxhole. Not wanting sympathy or to appear afraid, he was not about to complain to anyone.

Just offshore, Navy crews aboard small ships began launching illuminating flares that lit the battlefield. These auburn flares were designed to avert enemy infiltrators from attacking in the cover of darkness. Lying on his back, George was fixated on the fiery tail of each volley. At the apex of each salvo, the flare would burst into a brilliant white flame and remain aloft for about fifteen seconds as it swung effortlessly under a small parachute.

Settled in, George pictured how he would respond to the Banzai attacks that were expected during the night. Most veterans of the Pacific Theater told terrifying tales of these Japanese attacks, where they would affix their bayonets and scream "banzai" while running toward the enemy in desperation. Though the strategy usually failed to accomplish any significant military objective, it was viewed as an honorable way to die in Japanese military culture.

At 1900, several minutes had passed since that last illuminating flare, and suddenly George heard rustling footsteps in the sand. Within seconds, he heard men cursing and grunting as they struggled to defend themselves from a silent enemy attack. Grenade explosions were heard in the distance.

George poked his head slowly above ground level to look for the cause of the commotion, but it was too dark to see. The infiltrators were gone as quickly as they came. In the darkness, a tropical rain began to fall and men were heard calling out "corpsman" while others simply shouted in anger at the swiftness of the attack. It was later learned that the Japanese had stumbled across the lines established by E and D Companies, and had unknowingly fallen in the row of rifle pits.[3]

Destroyed Japanese planes discarded off the side of Motoyama Airfield #1

Illuminating shells, fired from supporting warships, light up the dark no-man's-land between the Japanese and American front lines... These lights were parachuted in from the sea every few minutes to prevent enemy infiltration

The rain continued to fall, with the noise of each drop hitting the sand seeming to drown out the sound of potential enemy attacks. After thirty minutes of acute listening, some men began to hallucinate hearing the footsteps of an attacking enemy soldier. Through the sound of gunfire and artillery shells, each man would hold his breath to listen more closely to any unfamiliar sounds. After determining its harmless origin, they would exhale slowly in relief.

During an illuminating flare, any movement above the ground level drew rifle fire from Japanese snipers. In the darkness, any noise could draw an enemy hand grenade. Alone in his foxhole, George was too frightened to sleep, and too stimulated on adrenaline to call off his vigil.

Just after midnight, the Japanese unleashed a horrifying attack on the regimental artillery headquarters within the Fox Company's perimeter. Salvo after salvo was launched at the tanks deemed the most significant threat to the Japanese defenses. Captain Caldwell recalls, "The Japanese artillery batteries started tearing us apart, you could hear the tank's metal… just sections of it… flying through the air, you could see it too, it was red hot. And a lot of it came flying over our heads."[4]

When the shelling ceased, George watched colorful tracer bullets fire directly into Japanese caves and fortified bunkers on Mount Suribachi. While the brilliant flares continued to bathe the field of battle, the swinging flares threw eerie shadows on rocks and bushes that appeared to give motion to these stationary objects.

Hour after hour, the flares were launched, and George's eyelids grew heavier. At 0200, he finally dozed off to sleep.

An hour later, George was suddenly awakened by a thud and sizzling noise in his foxhole. He was paralyzed with fear, believing an infiltrator had thrown a grenade at him. He hugged the edge of his foxhole in a futile attempt to get as far away from the object as possible. After several tense moments waiting for the explosion, he began to breathe normally again, realizing that the object was not going to detonate. He began probing the moist sand with his hands, but came up empty. As he lay thinking about what hap-

Tracer bullets from anti-aircraft guns ashore and aboard ships stab thru the black night at Iwo Jima, as American forces set up a barrage to repel a Japanese air attack on portions of the island held by Marines

pened, his heart stopped racing and the adrenaline subsided, but he couldn't go back to sleep.

By daybreak, enough light had peered over the horizon for George to find the object that caused all the excitement. He reached out and latched on to a chunk of shrapnel that had landed near him. It had hissed as it cooled in the damp sand. George thought how fortunate he had been to have avoided being hit by this fist-sized chunk of metal.

This gruesome scene was captured by combat photographer W. Newcomb
The original caption read: "Jap arm in the middle of Airfield #1,
no longer able to toss a grenade or fire a rifle."

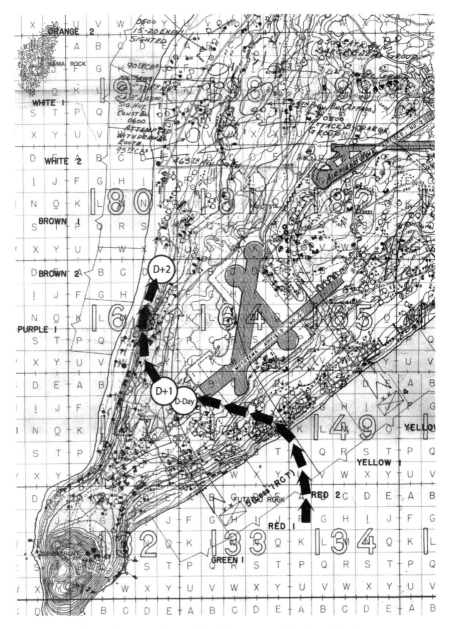

Approximate location of Fox Company on D+1 and D+2 as
indicated on an operations map

Chapter Ten

D+1 and D+2: The First Casualty

". . . Iwo Jima can only be described as a nightmare in hell."
— Robert Sherrod,
Combat Correspondent for Time-Life

When the Marines emerged from their foxholes the next morning, they arose to an overcast sky and a stiff wind that seemed like an omen for the first day after D-day or D+1. Debris and wreckage occupied almost every inch of the potential landing sites along the beach. DUKWs, tanks, half-tracks, landing craft, and cranes clogged vital landing lanes. The rising tide further complicated the cleanup efforts as soft sand and the churning undercurrent consumed the disabled vehicles. Even bulldozers couldn't loosen the sand's glue-like grip on the shell-torn wreckage strewn the length of the beach. Underwater demolition teams were summoned to eliminate the obstacles and open the beaches for desperately needed deliveries of ammunition and supplies.

Shore parties also worked tirelessly, striving to keep the supply trains open. Amphibious tanks were about the only vehicle that could scale the sandy terraces and reach solid ground without assistance. These odd-looking vehicles became an invaluable means of shuttling ammunition, water, and other supplies to the front lines.

Generals Schmidt and Smith faced a dilemma. Without reinforcements, the entire invasion could be crippled, as the relentless Japanese resistance continued to stifle American advances. The generals could also use the 3rd

Wreckage strewn across the beach threatened the success of the invasion

Marine Division, still in floating reserve, but with the beaches choked off, it had been difficult to land supplies, let alone an additional 20,000 men. To make matters worse, the weather conditions became so threatening that Marine commanders were forced to shut down beach operations temporarily due to a hazardous undertow and rapidly rising surf. At the end of D+1, the supply chain to the fighting men was dangerously insufficient, and casualty rates were even higher than on D-day.[1]

Clearing the beaches was imperative if this campaign were to succeed. Marine commanders ordered a redoubling of efforts to get—and keep—the beaches cleared. Marines toiled around the clock, enduring the incessant barrage of enemy mortar and artillery fire.

A second imperative was to secure Mount Suribachi and deny the Japanese their superior observation point from which they controlled the offensive. Camouflaged artillery, mortar, and rockets were the main source of enemy fire plaguing Marines who were trying to clear the beach or advance inland.[2]

Combating the Japanese offensive, the 28th Marine regiment continued their rock-by-rock, cave-by-cave assault on Mount Suribachi. With assistance from the big naval guns offshore, some progress was made up to the first shoulder of the hill. Still, camouflaged Japanese mortarmen tracked the advance of each patrol as it made its way up the slopes, the enemy were perfectly positioned to drop a shell on any cluster of Marines they targeted. Richard Wheeler, a rifleman with the 28th Marine regiment, described the predicament by saying, "The Jap mortarmen seemed to be playing checkers, and using us as the squares."[3]

While the 28th Marine Regiment inched its way up Mount Suribachi, George's 26th Marines were officially in division reserve, but continued to endure enemy mortar fire that threatened or prevented their movement as they pushed their lines forward. The front lines were a constantly moving target, and George scrambled from one shell hole to the next, trying to keep up with his unit. The 26th Marines were assigned to protect the left flank of the 27th Marines, whose men had spent the day pounding their way inland, so George's unit had to keep up with their movement.

Marines are advancing uphill, enveloping an enemy pillbox in the D-day fighting on Iwo Jima

Marines dug-in to avoid the enemy's mortar fire

Rumors of the 26th Regiment's imminent call to the front lines had been whispered from one Marine to another. George had seen the constant hail of rifle fire and hand grenades that left men beaten and bloodied as they were carried past him on litters and evacuated to the battalion aid station. He had also endured the hellish helplessness on the beach while pinned down, where he saw many friends die in hideously gruesome ways. He had seen dead men and pieces of flesh strewn across the landscape. But he had survived almost three days of furious battle conditions without yet treating a major battle wound from his own unit. Was it luck? Was it God's intervention, or something else beyond his control? Whatever had sustained him, he did not feel at ease with what might happen when his unit was sent to the front. He had managed to keep his emotions in check thus far, but his biggest worry was being immobilized by fear. Above all, George didn't want to be branded a coward among his Marine brothers who were performing so bravely under such horrible conditions. He wondered if he could still do his duty if they were sent to the front. He was soon to be tested.

Regimental commanders were attempting to coordinate an offensive and organize their men in a preassigned assembly area. Ongoing sniper fire grew so intense in the area that anti-sniper fire patrols were organized to help quell the attacks. These patrols suffered numerous casualties and were routed by persistent artillery and mortar fire. They returned to their units without success.[4]

Although each Marine felt relatively safe in his rifle pit, he was subject to constant machine gun and sniper fire. Fire from the enemy, from a network of tunnels, caves, and pillboxes, posed a constant threat to the Marines near the battlefront. Even worse than the large connected network of defense positions were the suicide holes built for sniper fire. Months before the Americans landed, the Japanese had created hundreds of spider holes. These concealed sniper locations were large enough for only one man, and were constructed of a modified 55 gallon drum. The Japanese would bury

Japanese sniper lies dead after being discovered in a spider hole

the drum, often on a 45 degree angle, with a hinged lid attached and the occupant inside. The entrance was camouflaged with grass and other vegetation that was planted months before the Americans landed. So the vegetation was established and blended into the natural habitat so well that most Marines couldn't see these spider holes until they were directly on top of them. Japanese soldiers would hide in these contraptions for days, knowing they would die there. Some packed hardtack or other biscuit-type foods, along with a canteen of water. Lying in wait in these highly camouflaged positions, the Japanese would allow the Americans to pass by and then quietly emerge to aim and shoot officers, corpsmen, and NCOs. George's first casualty was the result of this highly effective type of defense.

Second Lieutenant James W. Cassidy, of George's Fox Company, was inspecting the men in his platoon as they hunkered down in their foxholes. While scrambling from one group of Marines to another, a Japanese sniper, presumably in a spider hole, shot at the lieutenant, hitting him in the chest near his heart. Cassidy landed hard on the ground.

Without stopping to think, George crawled out of his foxhole on his stomach, his medical bag in tow, and scrambled to treat him. He was the first

Marine sights in his carbine on an opening to a Japanese pillbox

corpsman to reach Cassidy, but another Marine had already yanked off the jacket and vest. George noticed that the bullet's entry wound looked like a harmless purple-blue hole the size of a dime. There was little blood near the wound, so George probed his back, but couldn't find an exit wound.

The lieutenant faded in and out of consciousness. Working on his stomach, George feverishly unwrapped the battle dressing and threw the wrappers aside. The thick bandage of gauze had a trail of cloth on both ends. George quickly tied the ends of the dressing to secure the padding of gauze over the bullet hole. Ignoring the bullets that kicked up a spray of dirt nearby, he looked over his shoulder, hoping to find a team of stretcher-bearers. With no one in sight, George dragged the lieutenant by his armpits down the hill, out of the line of fire. When stretcher-bearers arrived minutes later, they carried Lieutenant Cassidy to a battalion aid station, where he later died.

After the lieutenant was evacuated, George felt numb. He realized that Cassidy had little chance of surviving, given the wound he had sustained internally. George was sickened not only by the memory of Cassidy bleeding to death, but by knowing he could do nothing more to prevent it.

As darkness fell, an intense barrage of mortar and artillery fire halted the advance of the 5th Division. The intensity of the barrage was so brutal that even the tanks were forced to halt their push forward.[5]

At 2130, Captain Caldwell received word from division headquarters that an enemy counter-landing was occurring on the western beach. Fox and Easy companies were sent to stop it.[6]

George joined the men in this platoon as they crawled through the night, toward the roar of crashing waves. As they approached, they could see shadows moving in the darkness, and could hear the clanking of weapons mixed with the muffled sound of men talking. The mortar section quickly set up their mortar tubes and traversed their weapons before letting loose a punishing barrage that blanketed the beach. When the mortars ceased, so did the activity on the beach. The next morning, twenty dead enemy soldiers were scattered on the sand or floated facedown in the surf.[7] No one ever determined whether this enemy activity was indeed a counter-landing or infiltration, but that didn't matter to the men of Fox Company. The Americans had experienced success for the first time on the island. They returned to the rifle pits they had prepared earlier that evening and buttoned down for the night.

As indicated by the beach attempt, the Japanese were growing bolder in their infiltration efforts. Now they were using their superior camouflaged positions to listen to conversations between Marines. Throughout the night, the Japanese would use the information they had overheard and attempt to trick the dug-in Marines to reveal their locations.

Earlier that night, Corpsman Roy Service had been loudly reprimanded many times for making several mistakes, and his name was called out in anger by officers and NCOs alike. His name was repeated often enough that Japanese infiltrators began mimicking those calls to harass the Marine.

"Service, come here right now," said a voice in the distance. The call was not in a familiar voice, so Corpsman Service listened closely and detected a Japanese accent in the pronunciation of his name. Throughout the night, the Japanese continued to shout "Service, where are you?" and "Damn it, Service, get over here." hoping to elicit some response from him.[8] Fortunately, Corpsman Service didn't respond, but hearing the enemy call his name was especially unnerving.

The close proximity of the Japanese to Marine conversations resulted in a compromise of the password "Chevrolet," a word selected to detect a Japanese accent. Watching closely for enemy infiltrators, PFC Thomas J. Farkas was out on patrol, guarding stretcher-bearers who carried wounded men back to the aid station. Not knowing he was out in front of his lines, he was startled when a man holding a gun approached his position. He challenged the shadowy figure to halt and reveal the password. He heard the person reply in a clear, American accent "Chevrolet." Farkas had been warned not to accept "Chevrolet" or "Ford" as the password. The men had been instructed to demand a second password, such as Plymouth, Buick or Oldsmobile.

Farkas stiffened his hold on his rifle and demanded another password. The man paused, not knowing how to respond. Farkas again demanded another password but was met with silence. Farkas realized that the man was not an American, so he confidently pulled the trigger on his rifle. The man fell backwards, hitting the ground with a thud. Farkas poised his finger on the trigger and was ready to shoot again, but the motionless figure remained still for several minutes. Confident the man was dead, he continued his trek back to his unit. When Farkas reported the incident to his platoon sergeant, he emphasized that the enemy had learned the password. When the morning came and light fell over the corpse, Marines nearby saw the dead Japanese man and sent word back to the command post that Farkas had indeed killed an enemy soldier.[9]

During the night, orders were received that 2/26 was assigned to pass through the lines currently being held by 3/27.[10] George didn't sleep much again, but nobody could sleep with the constant explosions of artillery and mortars shells breaking the night silence. He hunkered down in his foxhole and contemplated the situation of the coming day. After two and a half days of fighting, advances had yet to reach the first day's objectives, and supply shortages continued to plague the men fighting on the front lines. For the first time, Marines used the new M29 Weasel, a small tank-like vehicle with sturdy tracks, making it both rugged and agile over the island's terrain. It successfully shuttled water and vital equipment, like flame-thrower canisters, to the front lines. It also helped evacuate the wounded to aid stations in the rear.

Morning on D+3 found the dead and wounded piled up on the beaches, left there while landing craft struggled to get ashore to evacuate them. Within 60 hours, the Marines had suffered a whopping 5,300 casualties. During that time, just over 600 Japanese had been counted as dead, but Marine commanders hoped that many more dead Japanese had not yet been counted.

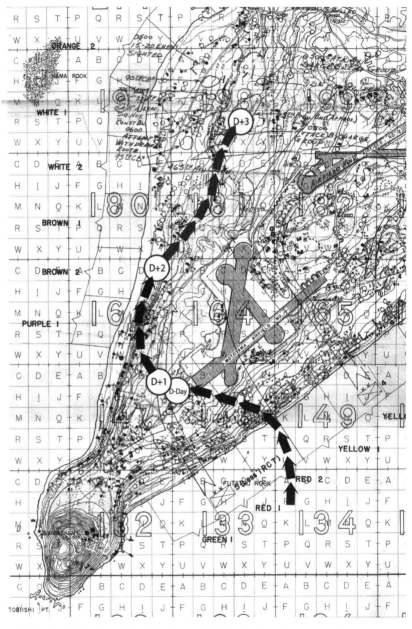

Approximate location of Fox Company on D+3 as indicated on an operations map

CHAPTER ELEVEN

D+3: THIS LOUSY, STINKING ISLAND

"In the last and final analysis, it is the guy with the rifle and machine gun who wins and pays the penalty to preserve our liberty."
—James Forrestal, Secretary of the Navy

On Thursday morning, D+3, a drenching rain and stiff wind made it even more difficult to move from one place to another. Mortar and artillery fire continued throughout the night, and yellow-orange illumination flares brightened the night sky. At the base of Mount Suribachi, the chilling wind and rain pierced the already miserable Marines who shivered in their foxholes.

The dank weather was not only dismal, but the cold rain made a gritty mush out of the ashy sand. It was difficult to walk in it, and crawling was worse because the volcanic grit wrecked rifle mechanisms and generally fouled their weapons. At 0500, Fox Company was again assigned to go on the offensive. Marine intelligence had identified a group of enemy soldiers hiding out in the sulfur pits near the western beach. George's 2nd platoon formed into a skirmish line and headed northwest, while the other platoons were sent forward.

Expecting to find fierce opposition, the platoon was surprised when they met limited resistance. With the help of a machine gun section commanded by 2nd Lt. Earnest Clark, the Japanese soldiers were caught completely off guard and annihilated.[1]

The rout lasted less than an hour, and the platoon returned to the assembly area minutes before the battalion was about to embark on a new assault toward 3/27 lines. This assault had been in the works for almost two days, but had been delayed multiple times. The forward line being held by 3/27 was about 75 yards shy of the 0-1 line, the imaginary line designating the first day's objective, and was marked by a road going east and west.[2]

Seeing the Marines prepare for their assault, the Japanese were ready. Enemy spotters watched the concentrations of Marines as the men of 2/26 changed positions with weary Marines of 3/27. Enemy mortar and artillery-men couldn't have planned a more tempting target, and they let loose salvo after salvo of mortar and artillery shells that landed directly into the large gathering of Marines.

The mortar barrage was so intense that it seemed it would never end. Shell bursts blasted men and equipment every few seconds. At times, several shells discharged simultaneously. Any Marine within ten feet of the concussion felt the air sucked from his lungs, and the deafening sound of the intensified blasts dazed his senses. Hot, sizzling shards of metal whizzed by in every direction with incredible velocity. The shrapnel ripped through flesh and bone like the pointed end of scissors through newspaper.

Joe Malone, George's platoon sergeant, was leading the platoon up a hill when an artillery shell landed at his feet. The blast sent him airborne, ripping away his right leg above the knee, his fingers on his right hand, and the right side of his face.

Fortunately, George was only seconds away, and he immediately crawled to him to attend to his wounds. The sergeant's dungarees still smoldered where the hot shrapnel had cut through the cloth of his fatigues, and what remained of his leg bled furiously. His blood-drenched stump was covered in the coarse volcanic sand, and it mixed with strands of thread from his dungarees. George quickly wrapped a tourniquet around the leg above the knee and pulled tightly to stop the bleeding. Sergeant Malone grimaced in pain. George pushed a thick battle dressing on the stump as he tried to wipe away the debris, but the dirt was embedded in the bleeding muscle tissue. George hastily wrapped gauze around the stump to help keep the battle dressing affixed.

He took out another battle dressing and applied pressure to the Sergeant's right hand, where only the thumb remained. He pushed the dressing directly into the exposed bones and muscle tissue, then wrapped it around his wrist and tied the ends together. Then he reached into his "unit-3" medical bag and grabbed a thin, clear tube containing a syrette of morphine, and inserted the needle into Malone's thigh. Within seconds, the Sergeant went limp and lost consciousness. George hurried to treat his facial wound where the blast had peeled away skin from the side of his face leaving teeth, gums and cheekbone exposed. Finally, he wrapped a battle dressing around the Marine's head to stop the bleeding. Seeing the platoon sergeant so mangled was frightening, and George realized that Malone could only survive if he could immediately be seen by the battalion surgeon.

Luckily, a litter crew was nearby, and George shouted at them to come over to his location to evacuate Sergeant Malone. Within minutes, the stretcher-bearers crawled over and lifted Joe gently onto the stretcher. Ignoring the bullets whizzing by, they ran with the sergeant back to the battalion aid station. George learned a few days later that Sergeant Malone had survived and was evacuated to a hospital ship headed for Guam.

While George was treating Sergeant Malone, his platoon continued to advance up the hill. Desperate not to be left behind, George scurried up the incline to find them.

While jumping from one shell hole to the next, he came upon a Marine wearing a flamethrower's canister on his back. He was aiming the hot end of the weapon toward the ground, and the pilot flame at the end of the barrel hissed menacingly.

Marine with flamethrower canister
advances under fire

George asked the Marine if he had seen his platoon, but before the Marine could answer two Japanese soldiers jumped out from a camouflaged gun position and charged directly at them. The Marine reflexively squeezed the trigger on his flamethrower, spraying the charging Japanese soldiers with a thick gel of flaming napalm. The enemy soldiers slowed their assault, but continued charging toward them. Finally overcome by the searing flames, both Japanese soldiers collapsed a few yards in front of them.

Wincing as they screamed in agony, George watched as the enemy soldiers were slowly consumed by the intense flames. He and the other Marine remained in the protection of a shell hole, fixated on the blackened figures, horrified and stunned at the sight. The burning corpses continued to crackle and smolder for several minutes more. By then, Japanese spotters noticed their location and had begun targeting it. They both jumped from their shell hole and ran to find protection further up the hill.

Sickened at the thought of what he had seen, George tried to block the event from his mind and focused on finding his platoon. Through the din of rifle and mortar fire, George listened closely. He heard the sound of someone moaning in pain. Straining his ear to listen, George saw a Marine several yards away lying on a ridge beyond the established front line. He crawled up to the Marine as quickly as he could. The man was lying on his back, writhing in pain as his blood-covered arms held his stomach. Lifting the Marine's shirt revealed the spot where bullets from a machine gun had peeled away the skin and visceral membrane, leaving the man's intestines exposed and falling from his abdominal cavity.

George thought back to his field medical training school and remembered that when internal organs were exposed, the wound was best treated by keeping them moist. He reached for a battle dressing from his medical bag and soaked the gauze with water from his own canteen. Gently he held the organs in place while he secured the bandage over the man's intestines. The Marine continued thrashing around in pain, and his pale complexion led George to treat him for shock.

George removed a morphine syrette from his medical bag and briskly poked the needle into the Marine's arm. Within a minute, the Marine stopped moaning and began to relax. George told him to stay where he was and not move until a stretcher team could be summoned to get him evacuated. The man nodded slightly in agreement, then George jumped from the shell hole, hoping one of the stretcher teams would soon find this wounded man.

The potent Japanese offensive continued to harass the Marines with almost every blast. George crawled down the hill into a small valley, hoping to see someone he recognized. He scrambled from one shell hole to the next until he found a wounded Marine from his platoon. After he quickly applied a battle dressing, George found stretcher-bearers that carried the wounded Marine back to an aid station.

Immediately, George again heard the call for a corpsman. He disregarded that he was going into the line of fire as he ran out to retrieve the wounded Marine. The man was hit in both his head and neck, and blood continued to spurt from his wounds. George quickly applied pressure to the gaping wound with a clean battle dressing. He slowed the bleeding enough to look over his shoulder for stretcher-bearers. He saw his friend Dean Keeley

Some of the less fortunate on the west side of the airstrip #1

nearby, and asked Keeley if he would stand by to help him lift the wounded Marine onto the stretcher. Keeley agreed. When the stretcher team arrived, George didn't recognize any of the men, supposing they must be replacements. Upon seeing the blood-soaked stretcher, one of the Marines turned to George and said, "I can't pick him up. Everything's covered in blood."

Impatient with the young Marine's refusal, Keeley pulled out his .45 caliber pistol, and pointed it directly in the stretcher-bearer's face. He said, "You either pick him up, or you're dead!" Seeing the seriousness in Keeley's face, the Marine quickly grabbed the handles of the stretcher and helped carry the wounded man away.[3]

George surveyed the battlefield again, looking for any wounded Marines he had missed. He continued to crawl up the hill until he found the young Marine whose stomach wound he had treated several hours earlier. The wounded Marine was awake and calm, but was eager to be evacuated before nightfall because he feared he would not make it through the night. George yelled for the stretcher-bearers, who immediately ran to the Marine and lifted him on the stretcher. He was taken to the aid station and spent the night in a field hospital near the beach.

2nd Battalion continued its attack on the ridge despite a chilling downpour. Enemy machine gun and artillery fire was the most intense the Marines had seen so far.[4] Then, without warning, four M4A3 (Sherman) tanks rumbled to the scene to support the Marine offensive. The tank commanders were asked to support 2nd Battalion in its push up the hill. When the tanks finally saw their predetermined target, they were not aware that 2/26 had advanced into the target area. Ignorant of the danger posed to their own men, the tank commanders blasted away with their 75-mm guns.[5]

Quickly realizing the deadly mistake, Marines pounded feverishly on the tank's sealed hatch to get the attention of tank commanders, but the barrage continued. NCO's screamed in the telephone system installed on the back of the tank, and after several deadly minutes, the shelling stopped. Several casualties were evacuated as a result of this friendly fire incident.[6]

Having treated and evacuated an uncounted number of casualties during the advance, George worked his way up the incline and finally recognized the men from his platoon. Though exhausted and covered in blood, he was happy to be reunited with the men he had been so frantic to find.

Despite heavy opposition, the men of 2nd Battalion had quickly chewed up over 500 yards, then stopped to reorganize. Because of the speed of their advance, they found themselves overextended and exposed on both the right and left flank. By late afternoon, they were forced to relinquish 500 yards of the hard fought real estate so they could "tie in" with the other regiments and dig-in for the night. At the end of D+3, casualties were significantly out of proportion to the gains achieved. Of the just over a thousand men in the 2nd Battalion, 120 were killed that day alone. Morale plummeted, more because they had to pull back for safety and had lost so many men than because of the drenching rain and continued heavy opposition. Morale was worse on this day than on any other day of the operation.[7] The Japanese continued to badger the Marines with incessant mortar and artillery fire throughout the night. And if that wasn't bad enough, orders were received during the night to prepare for an attack the next morning at 0730.

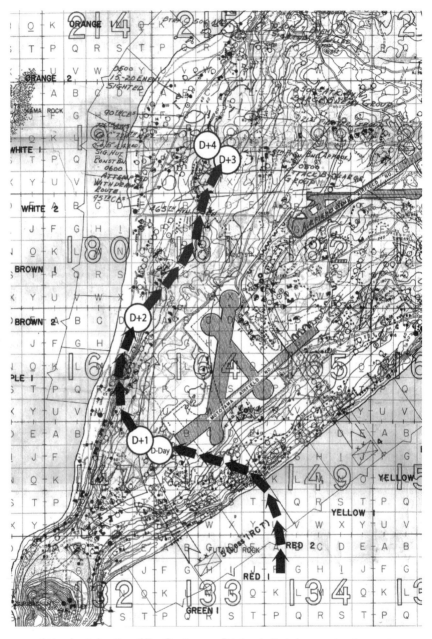

Approximate location of Fox Company on D+4 as indicated on an operations map

CHAPTER TWELVE

D+4: A SHIFT IN MOMENTUM

*"Each man should think of his defense position as his graveyard,
fight until the last and inflict as much damage to the enemy."*
—Lt. General Tadamichi Kuribayashi

George spent another wet, miserable night jostling with a Marine, trying to get comfortable in the foxhole. Each of them took a two-hour turn to sleep while the other stood watch, looking for Japanese infiltrators. For most Marines, sleep was an elusive luxury, but George was fortunate to doze off quickly during his two-hour sleeping shift.

By daybreak Friday, February 23, many rifles were victims of the rain and sand. The gritty mush found its way into rifle barrels, trigger mechanisms, and bullet chambers, rendering many useless. But supplies were scarce, and it was difficult to get weapons replaced, unless you took one from a dead man.

The Japanese continued to harass loading operations with artillery, mortar, and sniper fire, successfully stalling the supply line to the front and wreaking havoc on the beaches. Because of this, supplies to the front were getting critically low, and wounded men lay stranded on stretchers near the beach, waiting to be evacuated to the fleet. Some of the wounded were hit again as they lay on the beach, holding on until an empty landing craft was available. The weather continued to make any landings difficult, so both supplies into the front and evacuation of the wounded slowed to a crawl, despite shore parties working under fire around-the-clock to keep the beaches cleared. The ammunition shortages plagued mortar teams and prevented them from fully supporting the day's offensive.

At 0700, the regiment's planned attack was called off to accommodate the 3rd Marine Division's being brought up to the front lines.[1] By 0800, the rain had let up, and Fox Company was spread out along the western side of the island, awaiting orders.

Meanwhile, the offensive continued on Mount Suribachi. Capt. David Severance assigned Lieutenant Harold G. Schrier of 2/28 to select a patrol of 40 men he would lead up the mountain. They carried a 54" x 28" flag provided by 2/28 commander Lt. Colonel Chandler W. Johnson to raise at the summit.[2]

Throughout the island and offshore, men with binoculars could watch this group's ascent. George's friend Dean Keeley, dug-in on the north side of Airfield #1, heard whisperings from other men that some Marines were scaling Mount Suribachi. Keeley had picked up a pair of binoculars along the way, and was able to see the group of men start up the hillside.

He recalls: "I took these field glasses, and looked at the mountain, and sure enough, I could see them going up. So I watched them. It took about 45 minutes to go from the base to the summit. When they got up there, they fanned out, and I watched them, and I watched this flag go up. This was the first flag, which was the small flag."

Men cheered and ships sounded their whistles or sirens at the sight of the Stars and Stripes fluttering atop the highest point on the island. Captain Caldwell was hunkered down at the Company Command post, still dodging artillery fire, while this happened. Senior Corpsman Everett Kellogg noticed the flag, turned to Caldwell and said, "Look, there's the American flag waving on top of Suribachi." Captain Caldwell retorted, "I don't have time to look at that. We've got problems here."

The effect of the flag raising was immediate, causing many Marines' spirits to soar. Some men cheered, others felt a lump in their throat, and still others wept openly. Captain Thomas M. Fields of 2/26 D Company heard someone blurt out to look up at Suribachi. Just as he turned around, he saw the flag as it was hoisted up. His appreciation of the accomplishment was less about the symbolism and more about the strategic advantages. He recalls his first thought: "Thank God the Japs won't be shooting us down from behind any more."[3]

The raising of the U.S. flag on Suribachi had a different effect on the Japanese. Upon seeing the flag, many Japanese soldiers lost control of their senses. It was the first time an invader's flag had flown over what they considered traditional homeland territory. On the summit, Japanese soldiers abandoned the safety of their caves and fought ferociously against the American aggressors. Anticipating an offensive, Marines fanned out to meet their attack and successfully defended their positions on Suribachi's crater. But success for any Marine on Iwo Jima was short-lived. Of the 40-man patrol responsible for the first flag raising, thirty-six were killed or wounded in later fighting on Iwo Jima.[4]

Four hours later, a second patrol ascended Suribachi to preserve the historic smaller flag from souvenir hunters. Associated Press photographer Joe Rosenthal captured this event with what many believe is the most famous

A still photograph taken from the 16mm movie series of the Marines raising the second American flag on the summit of Mount Suribachi on Iwo Jima... Associated Press photographer Joe Rosenthal is standing nearby and is about to snap his famous photograph

With Mount Suribachi secure, Marines look north at the continued fighting

photograph of the war.[5] Both flag raisings boosted the morale of the Marines still struggling to take the island. The capture of Mount Suribachi was a huge step, but had come at a heavy cost. The 28th Regiment had taken Suribachi in less than five days, and at the end of D+4 had suffered more than 900 casualties.[6] But their work wasn't finished yet.

Once cleanup operations had eliminated the final vestiges of the enemy on Suribachi, the 28th's next aim was to support the 5th Division's push to the north. Unfortunately for the Americans, losing Suribachi didn't mean the Japanese had forfeited their only strategic observation point. Japanese artillerymen continued their relentless assault on any cluster of Marines they spotted.

At noon, 2/26th's Commanding Officer Lieutenant Colonel Joseph P. Sayers suffered shrapnel wounds to his arm and side and was evacuated from the front. At that point, command of 2/26 fell to Major Amedeo Rea, a rugged Marine who had won the Eastern collegiate boxing championship. As Rea assumed the command, he didn't know that his battalion would suffer more casualties on Iwo Jima than any other group on the island.

Throughout the day, George and his unit were on the defensive as Japanese forces made every attempt to prevent the Marines from organizing. George remained in his foxhole as much as he could because he didn't want to draw attention to himself. Even still, the mortar and artillery fire continued to land near him at a frantic pace. When he wasn't hunkered down in his foxhole, George followed his platoon as they helped resupply the front line units and clean weapons from the baneful sand and rain. The irony of being "in reserve" didn't escape the men behind the lines, as each Marine knew too well that each time he moved above his foxhole he could draw enemy fire. Though great were the perils of the daylight hours, darkness ushered in an even more terrifying threat of Japanese infiltrators.

General Kuribayashi's forces organized effective spoiling attacks, using large numbers of troops—some of whom reached the size of entire U.S. companies. These targeted, nighttime attacks were designed to retake lost ground, disrupt Marine offensive preparations, and harass the weary infan-

Corpsman gives brandy to victim of shock

trymen. Each night brought the threat of enemy infiltrators, although the effectiveness of these attacks waned throughout the campaign. On the front lines, Japanese soldiers were within hand-grenade distance of the dug-in Americans. Marines who simply whispered to each other risked revealing their location and having a grenade land in their foxhole. As the night wore on, exhausted Marines started to imagine hearing the sounds of enemy footsteps or conversations of enemy soldiers preparing their next attack. With each imagined or real sound, the surge of adrenaline flowed through their veins, and the mental and emotional pressure increased. Now they were fighting themselves as well as their enemy.

After five days of adrenaline overload and sleep deprivation, some men began to exhibit bizarre behavior. Corpsmen were trained to identify combat fatigue, and now they were seeing the symptoms in increasing numbers. Corpsman Richard E. Overton recalled seeing "facial muscles loose and jaws hanging slack as they stared at me with that dull look that men get when subjected to exhaustion. Their eyes seemed to fail to register what they were seeing. I could see fear, confusion, and exhaustion in their eyes and their grime covered faces were void of any expression."[7]

Combat fatigue cases were manifested in different ways. Some men became catatonic, others were unable to control their bowels, and still others became irrational or exhibited manic symptoms. These cases were difficult to treat, especially at night when careless movement could be suicidal. Corpsmen could do little else but tag victims as combat fatigue cases and hope they could hold out through the night. They could then be assisted to an aid station at daybreak.

At the end of D+4, a planned attack was delayed again, partially because the American offensive was stalled, waiting for reinforcements. Now that the 3rd Division was ashore, an additional 20,000 men were engaged in the battle. Confident of their superior numbers, Marine commanders planned an all-out attack for the next day.

Notwithstanding the day's setbacks, a change in momentum was palpable among the Marine brass, and they hoped that shift in the "Big Mo" would be sensed by the rank and file Marines. Having amassed their heavy "shock weapons" on a single front, they hoped to create a breakthrough the next day. By midnight, all Marines along the 5th Corps lines knew that tomorrow's offensive would commence at the signal of a rocket barrage.

In his foxhole that night, George, wet, grimy, and depleted, was trying to rest before the next day of combat. He was learning something about himself. Despite all he had seen and endured in five days of combat, he had not faltered or given in to fear. More important, he was keeping up with his Leatherneck buddies and was earning their respect. Though sleep was difficult, if not impossible, he settled in and waited for daylight.

Forward observers identify an enemy machine gun nest, and are collaborating to find the location on the operations map... These coordinates are sent to artillery and mortar sections who will then target the enemy position

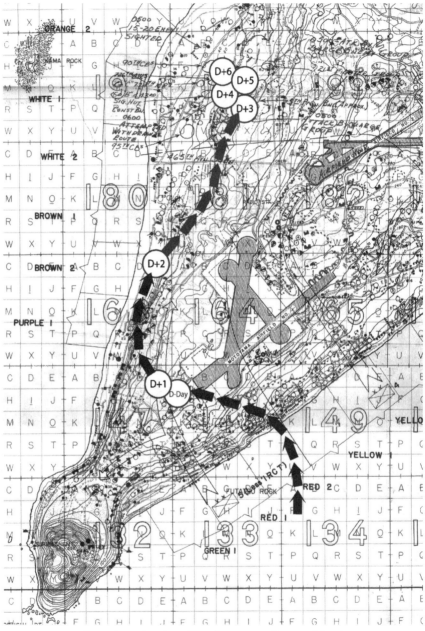

Approximate location of Fox Company on D+5 and D+6
as indicated on an operations map

Late Friday night, Fox Company had dug-in behind the lines, and George slept well throughout a relatively quiet night. His company was still officially in battalion reserve, and at daylight, they anticipated the signal for Easy and Dog companies of the 26th Marines to lead the attack.[1] But as Marine commanders prepared for the day's operation, they didn't realize that they were about to attack General Kuribayashi's principal defensive zone on the island.

The 21st Marines were sandwiched between the 24th Marines on the right, and the 26th Marines (minus Fox Company) on the left, running parallel to the western beach.

Forward line artillery outpost in front of a burned-out Japanese pillbox

Marines inspect Japanese dead heaped around a blasted gun emplacement

The morning's operation involved attacking the west-central defenses just north of Airfield #1 with the tanks of all three divisions ready to move. At 1330 hours, several trucks equipped with rocket launchers let loose a thunderous assault on the Japanese. The rocket launch was the signal to each division to begin its attack. As the rocket launchers scurried away from the battlefield, Marine artillery, Naval gunfire, and even air assaults began targeting the Japanese strongholds. Dust, debris, and smoke filled the air as Marines pressed forward in the attack. Tanks rumbled ahead, but were hobbled by anti-tank mines and stiff artillery fire. Despite the losses of several tanks, the Marines were still able to crush their way between Airfields #1 and #2 to create a passageway between both airfields.

At that point, and in spite of well-intentioned planning, the fighting quickly deteriorated into skirmishes between smaller units like companies and pla-toons. The airport runways were open killing zones for the Japanese who had a superior vantage point over the advancing Marines. Little progress had been made so far. The 21st Regiment (3rd Marine Division) on the right flank had reached the southern edge of Airfield #2, but 2/26 had advanced a whopping 500 yards to the left of the 21st Regiment. To the right of 2/26, 2/27 faced stiff opposition from the entrenched Japanese and couldn't keep up with 2/26's advances. The length of 2/26's advance created a bulge in the front lines and made their positions difficult to defend.

As daylight dimmed, the job of consolidating the lines became almost impossible. Not only were men spread out across a loose front line, but Japanese mortar and sniper fire continued, making the process of unifying forces even more difficult. Because of the huge bulge in the line, Fox Com-pany was called in to consolidate the front lines, spacing their foxholes far enough apart to fill gaps in the lines established during the day.

Supply problems continued to plague the commanders of the front line troops. The choppy surf still pounded the beaches, preventing cargo de-liveries from landing. With the capture of Mount Suribachi, most of the harassing fire had stopped, but now the weather was slowing down beach operations. Despite little, if any, unloading of cargo, shore parties had suc-ceeded in laying down steel traction matting to help cover the beach exits and allow vehicles a firm footing to reach solid ground inland.

The reality of short supplies on the front lines forced officers to relax their orders that all Marines remain in their foxholes. It was obvious that with-out nighttime replenishment, the men on the front lines would face severe shortages of water and ammunition. "Carrying parties" were organized to transport critical supplies to front line troops, but those men were under constant attack from rifle and mortar shells. Japanese snipers were particu-larly effective in shooting stretcher-bearers, a group that also suffered heavy casualties throughout the night.

By Sunday morning, February 25, (D+6) the day's planned attack was again postponed. This time, the reason for the delay was to give the 3rd Division time to advance to the lines established by the 26th Marines.

While George's platoon mates cleaned their rifles and prepared for the "jump-off" for the day's attack, George remained in his foxhole. Like most Marines in company reserve, he hoped he wouldn't be called on to transport ammunition or water up to the lines. Even so, he was willing to go anywhere he was asked to, despite his desire to remain safe in his foxhole.

George had no rifle to clean because he had given away his carbine a few days earlier. He had realized that he needed both hands to treat the wounded, and it was too difficult to carry both his carbine and his medical bag. Then, as if he needed further convincing, a day or so later he had to jump from his foxhole to get away from a mortar round. As he jumped away, the barrel of his carbine caught on a branch and pulled him to the ground. Luckily, he avoided injury, but when George found a BAR man whose weapon was destroyed, he gladly gave the Marine his carbine.

The day was unusually quiet, despite the occasional "whoosh-whoosh" of the huge 360mm mortar rounds that the Japanese would launch. George learned on the first day that these tumbling mortars, known by some as "Burping Betties," would make an unmistakable noise that was quickly recognized. Once they heard the telltale "thump" of the mortar's launch, Marines would quickly look skyward, locating the tumbling projectile to determine its trajectory. If it was coming in their direction, they scrambled to avoid being at the receiving end of this huge explosion and the resulting huge crater.

Japanese "Burping Bettie" or spiggot mortar

That evening at dusk, George heard a "Burping Bettie" land near a small concentration of Marines. Fortunately, the soft, loose sand had absorbed much of the impact of the explosion. But at the bottom of the crater, Marines coming on to the scene noticed a hand protruding from the soft sand. Moments later a dark haired man emerged coughing and gasping for air. A Marine jumped to the bottom of the crater with his gun pointed at the man. He could see the person's almond-shaped eyes, and he yelled up to his platoon leader, "We got one!"

George watched as other Marines jumped to the bottom of the crater and probed the man with their bayonets to encourage him to dig out more quickly. The Marines were cautious because they had been warned of Japanese soldiers being booby-trapped with grenades and demolitions attached to their bodies. They had also heard reports of the Japanese donning uniforms of deceased Marines.

As the dark haired man emerged, Marines shouted questions at him, but his responses were unintelligible. Satisfied that they had captured an enemy soldier, two Marines were assigned to escort the POW to the rear echelons for interrogation.

With his hands above his head, the POW arrived at Division Headquarters. He made several pleas for the Marines to believe that he was an American. After several tense hours, a Marine from his company finally identified the man as a fellow Marine from the Navajo tribe.

It was later learned that the hapless Marine had been assigned to duty as a stretcher-bearer and was lost when the spigot mortar landed. His limited English skills, compounded with his accent, and his fear of being shot resulted in his inability to communicate. Fortunately, he was not harmed and was returned to his unit.[2]

After several days under heavy mortar fire, the Japanese were less inclined to harass the Marines with their mortars and artillery. The night was relatively calm, and George dozed off quickly in his foxhole. The previous six days had tried his mettle; the next seven were to prove him further.

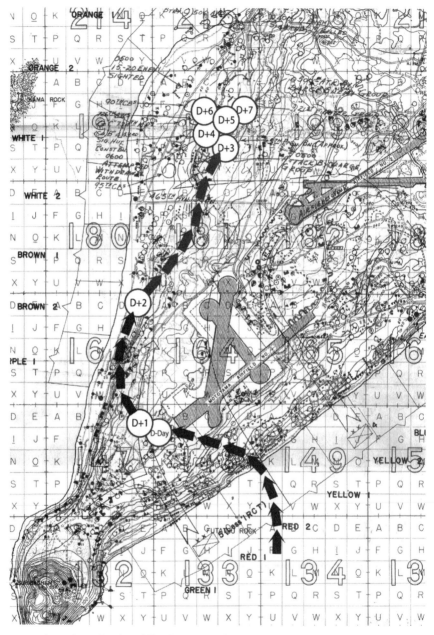

Approximate location of Fox Company on D+7 as indicated on an operations map

CHAPTER FOURTEEN

D+7 A.M.: THE CRUCIBLE

George woke before sunrise to the sounds of the ever-present artillery and mortar fire. During the night, two Japanese soldiers armed with Nanbu pistols had attempted to sneak past the patrols of the 27th Regiment, but they were summarily killed.[1] The Nanbus were highly prized by the Marines, and were quickly snatched up by two lucky souvenir hunters.

The jump-off time was set for 0800, but Fox Company was still to remain in reserve unless otherwise needed. George used the time to fill his unit-3 medical bag with battle dressings and other supplies. He also packed a few hand grenades because he heard how valuable grenades had been in close quarter fighting in previous days.

George pulled out his KaBar (long blade knife) and peeled open a can of scrambled eggs from a K ration. The key for the can was useless because the metal tab used to twist it open had broken off. A shortage of supplies meant that all the preferred C rations had already been eaten, and the tasteless, rubbery K rations were all that remained. George didn't care what he ate; he wasn't really very hungry, but he knew he had better eat something to maintain his strength for what could be a busy day ahead.

As the jump-off time approached, George concluded that the signal for the attack was again to be a rocket barrage, since he saw several rocket trucks getting into position. Each truck could launch 36 rockets with each salvo, and a salvo lasted only a few seconds. Reloading could take upwards of ten minutes, and rocket crews usually fired only one salvo. In a very un-Marine-like manner, the crews would fire their rockets, hop in their trucks and scamper away to find shelter.

Marine rockets on reconnaissance trucks are fired at the Japanese...
It is a hit-and-run process as the Japanese aim in the direction of the rocket's
position and within seconds, the enemy barrage arrives to knock out the trucks

This act of turning-tail was not lost among the Marine infantrymen who often derisively remarked that the rocket crews were guilty of desertion under fire.[2]

At 0715, Naval guns began to pound the pillboxes and cave openings in 5th Division's zone of action. Not long thereafter, Marine artillery began to supplement the Navy's attack. Just as expected at 0800, George watched from his foxhole as the bright flashes of the rocket barrage began, and he heard the rapid fire "swoosh" of the rockets leaving the launch tubes.

The smell of cordite wafted across the barren landscape, and individual Marines began leaping from their rifle pits. Some Marines fired their weapons at the pillboxes and cave entrances, hoping to connect with the ever-hidden enemy. As they began their advance, machine gunfire cut down several Marines within seconds. Watching in fear of meeting the same fate, other Marines remained in their foxholes, firing their weapons at targets of opportunity. As the attack progressed, Marine artillery rounds scored a direct hit on a pillbox, allowing Marines to advance a few yards. They repeated the process again and again, progressing slowly and deliberately forward.

After two hours of constant exchanges of mortar, artillery, and machine gunfire, the 2nd Battalion had advanced only 50 yards and suffered significant casualties. Major Amadeo Rea, commander of the 2nd Battalion, decided he had seen enough, so he decided to try another tactic.

Just before 1000 hours, Captain Frank Caldwell was ordered to take Fox Company forward and pass through the lines being held by the beleaguered Easy Company.[3] George followed his platoon leader as they jumped into a rifle pit where a Marine was firing at a pillbox. When the Marine realized he was being replaced, he stopped firing, looked right and left, and waited for the right opportunity to jump from the hole and crawl to a shell hole behind him. Within minutes, he and what remained of Easy Company were off the front lines, resting in the relative safety of battalion reserve.

Colonel Joseph Sayers, the architect of the 2nd Battalion strategy, had purposefully held Fox Company in reserve for such a circumstance. Although Colonel Sayers had been evacuated on D+4, Major Amadeo Rea, now at the helm of 2nd Battalion, understood the strategy and used a similar tactical

D+7: Members of Fox Company, 2nd Battalion, 26th Marines
advance toward the O-2 phase line

approach. His plan was to capitalize on Fox Company's natural competitiveness to prove they were as prepared for the task assigned as Dog or Easy Companies, who up until this time had seen most of the front line duty.[4]

Fox Company was positioned to move ahead, but visibility had worsened as a foggy haze blanketed the island. As if on cue, when Captain Caldwell gave the signal to move ahead, a light rain began to fall, and the combining mist over the battlefield resembled a Hollywood movie set.[5]

The Japanese resistance was fierce as their reinforced positions initially stalled Fox Company's attack. But within an hour, the Marines had learned how to coordinate their attacks and methodically eliminate a target, thus ridding themselves of several key Japanese emplacements. Or so they thought.

Just as the Marines began to gain momentum, the enemy would scramble underneath the island to one of the miles of connecting tunnels and return to a concrete pillbox that the Marines had believed to be secure. Consequently, Fox Company, suddenly attacked from the rear, suffered several casualties from machine gun and rifle fire.

Having to retake these positions, Fox Company learned quickly and began to use bazookas and hand grenades to neutralize the caves and reinforced

A 2nd battalion, 26th Marine infantryman advances past Marine tanks which are firing at the slope in the background... The slope contains Japanese machine guns

pillboxes, especially when they were reentering a previously secure area. As they neared a Japanese position, hand grenades were tossed into the small opening, and the resulting explosion usually eliminated the enemy.

It wasn't long before Fox Company was making tremendous progress against the once intractable Japanese defenses. Yet despite their advances, the Japanese continued to exact a deadly toll on the persistent Marines. As the 2nd platoon crossed a flat, acre-size area, the ever-patient Japanese commanders waited for the right moment when the Marines were most vulnerable and then suddenly attacked with an intense barrage of mortars and machine guns. Within seconds, several Marines lay wounded and helpless, unable to move and still vulnerable to the ongoing shower of exploding mortar shells.

George had concentrated on staying close to his platoon as they progressed northward adjacent to the other company units. But as he turned around during the attack on the 2nd platoon, he saw up to 15 wounded Marines scattered in the flat, open area that was still being slammed with mortar and artillery fire. Through the noise, he heard their screams of pain mixed with calls for a corpsman to help them.

D+7 at 0900 hours: "F" Company, Second Battalion, 26th Marines, advances under fire toward the O-2 Phase line

George couldn't ignore their pleas for help. He disregarded the exploding mortars that continued to pound the area. His friend Eddie Monjaras was the corpsman for the 2nd platoon, and George feared the worst had happened because Eddie wasn't there treating the wounded; Eddie would be there if he were able. Without hesitating, George crawled on his hands and knees into the line of fire and began to treat the wounded Marines.

Within seconds, he had crawled to the closest wounded Marine and struggled to drag him to a shell hole. George could see blood gushing from a puncture wound on the man's thigh, so he ripped open a sealed battle dressing and pushed gauze into the wound to stop the bleeding. When he had finished treating the leg wound, he quickly crawled on his stomach to the next Marine.

With so many wounded men, George first focused on attending to the most critical injuries. Some Marines were missing limbs, others had shrapnel wounds. Crawling to a second man, George quickly tied a tourniquet above his missing leg and tightened it carefully to stop the bleeding. As George finished with that man's injury, he crawled over to treat a third Marine with

One of three Marine tanks fires at a Japanese pillbox on the right flank of 26th Marines in their advance on the O-2 Phase Line

a shrapnel wound. George quickly cleared the dirt from the exposed flesh and applied a battle dressing to the bleeding area.

After each task was finished, he crawled from one casualty to the next. Hugging the ground to create the lowest profile he could manage, George ignored the intense explosions from mortar shells that continued to rain around him. Without stopping, he continued his quest to treat every wounded Marine in the area.

After treating his sixth or seventh casualty, he came across the familiar face of his friend Eddie Monjaras. George quickly crawled over to Eddie, who was hit badly in the chest and stomach.

Fortunately, Eddie was not fully conscious. George feverishly cleared away the jacket to assess the wound. He sucked in his breath. Just one look at the injury made George realize the severity of the wounds. He could see his best friend's intestines and vital organs exposed, and with each labored breath, the blood oozed freely from the skin that was ripped away in the blast. In the minutes it took to treat the other Marines, Eddie had lost a great deal of blood, soaking his dungarees with red. George gently pressed the bandage on the dark, red muscle and visceral tissue surrounding the wound before he quickly opened one of his last remaining syrettes of morphine to insert in Eddie's arm. Within a few seconds, Eddie's breathing had relaxed, and George patted his arm as he promised he would be OK. Still, he knew that Eddie's chances were not good as he summoned the stretcher-bearers. Within minutes, Eddie was being carried to an aid station. That was the last time he saw his friend alive, but George wasn't thinking of that. He had more wounded to attend to.

The overhead machine gunfire had stopped or at least George didn't notice it any longer. The mortars continued to land at a steady pace, but were somehow exploding far enough away that the shrapnel missed him.

After Eddie was evacuated, George continued to hear the call for "corpsman," and he faithfully performed his duty. At the end of twenty minutes of intense mortar shelling, George was treating his fourteenth and final casualty in this open killing field. He helped roll the wounded Marine onto a stretcher and watched the stretcher team dodge mortar shells as they hefted their comrade to an aid station at the rear of the lines.

Depleted, George crawled back to safety and scrambled to rejoin his platoon. Some of the men in his unit were shaking their heads in amazement, having watched this amazing act of courage. Without stating it, they knew they had witnessed one of those unexplainable phenomena on the battlefield. No one could explain how or why George survived almost 20 minutes exposed to the intense mortar barrage.

George collapsed, exhausted, into a shell hole and tried to catch his breath. Soon he began to replay the recent events in his head. It slowly dawned on him that he had somehow evaded countless mortar shells and treated fourteen Marines without as much as a scratch. The realization shocked him like a splash of ice water over his head. George rested his face in his hands and began to shake. He lay there in the hole for several minutes, but didn't have long to catch his breath. His platoon again started to advance. Eager to stay with his unit, he jumped from the safety of the shell hole and continued to seek cover.

The sloped sandy soil was subtly becoming steeper slopes, cliffs, and ravines. The increasingly rocky terrain concealed cunningly disguised gun emplacements and machine gun nests not discovered until someone was hit.

Looking up the hill to the east, George could see the discouraging complex of ridges and cliffs, with a large hill looming over the difficult terrain. The hill became known as Hill 362A, named for its altitude above sea level. Strangely, three hills of the same height existed on Iwo Jima, and they were distinguished by the Marines simply as Hill 362A, B, and C.

As they approached a hill, PFC Jack Russell of Ogden, Utah, had spotted an artillery piece on a railcar hidden inside the hill behind a camouflaged cave opening. Unexpectedly, it would emerge from the cave and fire its huge shells into a group of Marines, and then retreat within the cave. He watched the well-camouflaged gun several times, until he had memorized the bushes and other features, and could pinpoint its location. Just then, a group of five tanks came up from the rear.

Russell was asked to bring the tanks over, although they were now several hundred yards away. He ran across the open terrain amidst rifle and mortar fire to catch up with the tanks. Out of breath, he reached for the telephone on the rear of the lead tank and told the tank commander, "We need help straight ahead, on the hillside there; they've got an artillery gun that comes out on rails, a big one, and it's kicking our butts." [6]

Using the machine guns on the lead tank, Russell directed its gunfire with the help of the tracer rounds. When the bright tracer rounds landed on the exact location, he hollered to the tank commanders, "You're on it...now pour it to 'em!"

Just then, the three tanks in front, as well as the two in the rear, began to pound the mountainside with their big 75-mm shells. Russell, having no place to hide but behind the tanks, felt the concussion of each shell as it burst from the tank's big guns. The shells ripped into the Japanese artillery piece, and within seconds, it was silenced for good.

In front of the tanks was a dead Marine, who had fallen several feet beyond the end of the tank's 75-mm gun. With each shell, Jack watched as the concussion of each blast would blow the dead man's shirt over his head. Russell, unprepared for the intensity of the blasts, was deafened for hours, and his ears continued to bleed throughout the remainder of the day.[7]

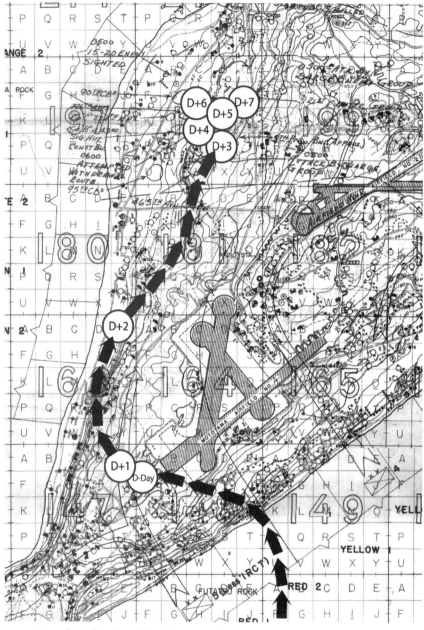

Approximate location of Fox Company on D+7 as indicated on an operations map

CHAPTER FIFTEEN

D+7 P.M.: MY JOB...NO MORE...NO LESS

The men of Fox Company were making significant progress, despite the challenges of the ravines and rocky terrain. As they inched their way up the incline, suddenly machine gun fire rang out, and everyone fell to the ground. Both the 1st and 2nd platoon were ordered to pull back off the hill to regroup. In the confusion, George began to climb back down the hill when he noticed two wounded Marines lying motionless in the sandy dirt. He crawled over to take care of them, but after one look at their wounds, he knew that both had been killed outright. Looking around for the quickest route back to his unit, George resumed crawling down the hill.

Suddenly, George heard a thud next to his head. Before he could react, a hand grenade exploded just a foot or so in front of him, and the concussion from the blast went directly by his face. Fortunately, the soft sand swallowed the bulk of the blast, and most of the grenade fragments flew skyward above George's head. He did catch several pieces of shrapnel in his face, just missing his right eye. Both stunned and dazed by the blast, George struggled to regain full consciousness. He could feel the searing pain of grenade fragments ripping his skin as warm blood ran down his face. Unable to move or make any effort to find shelter, he just lay there and hoped he wouldn't be hit again,

When several minutes passed, he finally gathered his wits and made a clear decision of what he should do. His right eye was blinded, and his face continued to bleed from the puncture wounds. It occurred to him to stop the bleeding, and he pulled out a battle dressing, wrapped the gauze ends around his head and covered his right eye. He quickly looked around for a place to hide and began inching down the hill to find his platoon.

After several more minutes, becoming fully aware of the danger he was in, he increased his pace and moved more quickly down the incline. Seemingly out of nowhere, George heard the call for a corpsman. To his left, he could see a wounded Marine lying 30 yards away. As he crawled in the man's direction, a grenade landed near the wounded Marine, then was followed by another, and another. George stopped crawling as he tried to assess the situation. It was then he saw a Japanese soldier emerge, throwing a fourth grenade from a cave opening on the hill. Realizing his only weapon was his .45 pistol, he yelled down to two other Marines in his platoon.

While enemy machine gun bullets whip the branches over their heads, Marines with an empty stretcher pass a dead Japanese soldier as they run for the next bit of cover

"Throw me up a grenade," George yelled. Promptly two men lobbed unarmed grenades in George's direction. He grasped a grenade in his hand and inched his way back up the hill toward the fallen Marine. A Japanese grenade landed a few feet behind George, and he felt the stinging sensation of shrapnel gouging into his buttocks and legs. But he continued to crawl and winced as two more grenades exploded near him, propelling even more metal fragments into his already tender backside. He ignored the stinging and continued crawling on his stomach toward the chasm above him.

As he approached the opening where he had seen the enemy lob the grenades, he glanced down to see a hole measuring two feet wide and six feet deep. Looking closer, he could see the tunnel opening, where the Japanese soldier would jump out, lob a grenade, and scurry back inside to safety.

Combat photographer Bob Campbell came upon this dead Japanese soldier

Trying to guess when the Japanese soldier would emerge again to lob another grenade, George pulled hard on the grenade's pin, pulling at the ring, but it didn't move. Puzzled, he noticed that the pin was bent as a safety precaution, and George didn't realize it until after he had tried to pull it out. Lying on his stomach, he calmly pulled out his KaBar, straightened the pin, then yanked on it to arm the grenade.

He was so close to the enemy soldier he contemplated using his .45 pistol, but since he was holding an armed grenade, he counted to two, and dropped it. Just as he dropped the grenade, the Japanese soldier jumped out of the tunnel opening, only to have the grenade explode and kill him instantly.

With one eye covered in gauze, he tilted his head so he could see with his good one. He found the wounded Marine and dragged him down the hill to treat him. The Marine was a large man, bulging with muscles, and weighing well over 200 pounds. His leg was torn apart leaving the bones of his calf exposed and bleeding. Working on his stomach, George pressed on the wound with a battle dressing causing the man to scream. Working as fast as he could he had the Marine bandaged and ready for evacuation within minutes. But as he looked around, George could see no stretcher-bearers and he could not lift his head any higher because of the grazing machine gunfire that continued to fly overhead.

He told the Marine he would need to crawl down the hill on his own, in order to get him evacuated. Determined, the wounded Marine reached forward with his arms, but he yelped in pain at the slightest movement of his broken leg.

Frustrated that he couldn't get the Marine evacuated by himself, both George and the wounded Marine lay on the ground waiting for the stretcher-bearers. Several minutes later, a lone Marine crawled up the hill with a stretcher, and the two of them rolled the wounded man onto it. Carefully, they dragged him down the hill, away from the line of fire.

George crawled back down to a ridge and paused to catch his breath. He wanted to catch up to his platoon, which continued to advance toward the most dominating feature of the terrain, Hill 362A, looming just 800 yards away. He trudged ahead for a few minutes until he heard the familiar voices of men from his platoon crouched in a shell hole. One of the men was Pharmacist Mate 3rd Class George Long, a fellow corpsman. George dashed over and leaped in the hole where they huddled.

As they contemplated their next move, a Marine yelled, "Long, someone needs a corpsman down there." He was pointing to the small ravine where George had been earlier.

Long replied, "You're crazy if you think I'm going down there."

Frustrated, the Marine yelled at Long, "Wahlen's already been down there for the past half hour… get down there and help that Marine."

Both George and the reluctant George Long crawled down the hill to find and treat the wounded Marine. Halfway down the hill, Long yelped, "I'm hit, I'm hit." George crawled a few feet up the hill and lifted the bloody sleeve of Long's shirt. The grazing wound bled for a few minutes as George bandaged it.

For over an hour, the two men treated one casualty after another until their medical supplies were exhausted and they could do no more.

As they sat in the protection of a shell hole, they realized that one of them would need to retrieve more medical supplies. Holding rank on Long, George asked him to go back to the Company command post (CP).

Long replied, "I'm not going back there."

George answered, "Well, I'm your senior, and I'm telling you to go back."

Long refused again saying, "If you're senior, then you go back."

After arguing for several minutes, George realized that Long was not going to cooperate and they still needed supplies. Frustrated and angry, George peered above the shell hole to find the quickest path back to the CP. He leaped up and ran down the hill, jumping this way and that to avoid being an easy target for a Japanese sniper.

Once he thought he was far enough away from the line of fire, George stomped his way to the CP, mumbling to himself about Long's insubordination. When he arrived at the command post, he was greeted by Captain Caldwell, who asked, "So Doc, how's the fighting going on up there?"

Frustrated, tired, and forgetting he was talking to his commanding officer, George quipped, "Why don't you go see for yourself."

The Captain just smiled at the remark, but looked curiously at George, who was covered in blood from lifting wounded men and had a swollen face that was bandaged and bloody.

"Doc, you look pretty beat up. Get yourself down to the aid station and get yourself looked at," Caldwell ordered.

Fearing he would be evacuated, George replied, "I'm not leaving. I just came back for supplies." George hastily grabbed several bandages, battle dressings, and other supplies, stuffed them in his medical bag, and walked away to return to his unit.

At 1500 hours, a small spotter plane noticed a group of enemy soldiers retreating from the rapidly advancing Marines. Fox Company, in conjunction with other elements of the 2nd Battalion, had been so successful in their attack that they had forced the Japanese from their honeycombed caves and tunnels. Unaccustomed to being exposed above ground, the Japanese resistance consisted only of small arms fire as they attempted to reposition several artillery pieces. This was the first time on Iwo Jima that Japanese soldiers were seen repositioning above the ground.[1]

The Marines pounded their positions with mortars and artillery, sending the Japanese scurrying around to find protection from the American barrage. The route of the vulnerable Japanese had a palpable effect on morale, "for no man likes to fight something he cannot see, and the sight of running Japs was, if nothing else, reassuring."[2]

As with any skirmish, the Japanese responded with artillery and mortar fire of their own. Among the casualties was Corporal Harold W. Crabtree, a gung ho Marine from Dog Company that almost everyone in the battalion knew and respected. Both he and his brother Luther had been together in the same unit since they had enlisted in Ohio two years ago. Luther had watched in horror as his brother fell. Panic evolved into dread as he saw his brother in the far distance, lying motionless.

"Get up… Harry…get up," Luther pled to himself, hoping he could will his brother to safety. It was not to be, though. Harold died, unable to be treated because the lines had adjusted during the battle, leaving his body well within Japanese lines.

The Crabtrees, along with PFC William C. Erler, had been a trio since boot camp. Erler looked at Luther and said, "We can't leave him out there." They convinced Captain Thomas Fields to stop the attack so they could retrieve Harold's body. Permission was granted to direct several .81 caliber smoke shells across the lines, where two Japanese pillboxes intersected their lines of fire. Erler and two other privates scrambled forward with stretchers and returned Crabtree's remains, as well as those of several other Marines nearby. Suddenly, the smoke screen dissipated, and as they carried Harold's body to the rear echelon, the war resumed. It was a surreal experience that few, if any, could forget. [3]

For the Japanese, prospects were growing worse by the hour. The 5th Division, led by Fox Company, had progressed almost 300 yards in less than 12 hours —a huge gain by Iwo Jima standards, and the backbone of the Japanese main line of defense had been bent, if not completely broken. During the day's attack, the men of 2/26 managed to capture the two re-

"Time Out: A corpsman has just completed caring for a wounded Marine, and is trying to get the gumption to look for his gear. He doesn't know how many Marines he has treated, nor does he know their names. He is cold, wet, dirty, and couldn't tell you if he has changed his socks, brushed his teeth or even washed his hands since the battle started." By Robert D. DeGeus, Corpsman F/2/26 on Iwo Jima. Watercolor

maining water wells the Japanese possessed.[4] From this day on, the Japanese would survive only on their existing rations or rainwater.[5]

The water situation was so desperate that at 2245 hours, an estimated 300 Japanese soldiers were spotted by an OY-2 observation plane preparing for a massive infiltration to regain the wells. In the moonlight, naval guns, in coordination with the entire 5th Division artillery units, began pounding the enemy position. At the end of the barrage, almost 600 rounds had landed on the disorganized Japanese. An untold number of Japanese soldiers were killed, an ammunition dump was set ablaze, and three artillery pieces were destroyed.[6]

The late night attack had capped off a successful day for Fox Company in terms of yards gained. Jumping off at 1000 hours, their spirited attack resulted in the destruction of enemy positions, including reinforced pillboxes, machine gun nests, and several mortar positions along the way. In terms of flesh and blood, Fox Company had suffered its worse day yet. By nightfall, George had treated more than 20 of the 49 casualties that day, and 18 men were listed as killed in action.[7] Of the 250 men who had landed on the island, Fox Company had already lost almost one-third of its fighting capability.

George was only a few feet away from the next foxhole. With two men in each foxhole, many Marines remained vigilant in trading watch duty every two hours. Some men, despite their best intentions, were too exhausted, and drifted off to sleep. George rested fitfully during his turn to sleep, and he kept his .45 pistol ready, hoping he wouldn't need to use it.

George and his platoon sergeant shared the duties of digging a foxhole that night. Just after midnight, George heard that Fox Company and the entire 2nd battalion were to be relieved by the Marines of 1/27 that morning at 0800. They welcomed the good news, but had little energy to celebrate, as they could only stare blankly into the moonlit battlefield.

As George took his turn standing watch, his thoughts raced. He imagined how pitiful he must appear; his uniform was filthy and caked in blood, much of it his own. His muscles were shaking from fatigue and his face was still swollen, limiting his sight to mostly one eye.

George was no longer concerned about acting cowardly in the face of battle. He had proven to himself that he was as willing to fight as much as any Marine in his company. Although he was glad he had not faltered throughout the day, he figured that what he had accomplished was no more heroic than what anyone else in his unit had done. He had done his duty. No more…no less.

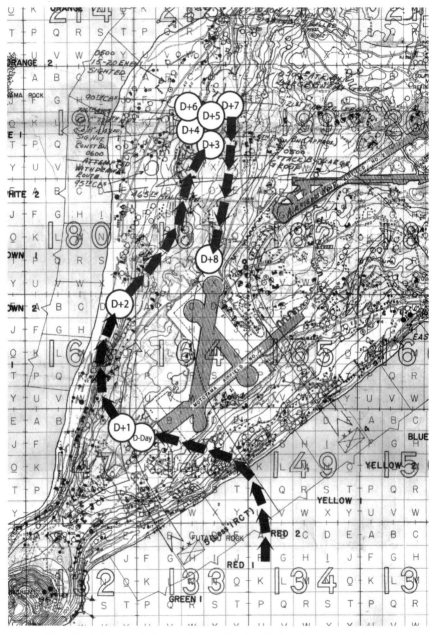

Approximate location of Fox Company on D+8 as indicated on an operations map

Chapter Sixteen

D+8: Regimental Reserve

The rustling of enemy soldiers could be heard in the distance throughout the night. Observers reported seeing the Japanese retrieving their dead and wounded from the devastating route of the failed infiltration attempt.

The men of 2nd Battalion, 26th Regiment had suffered several casualties during the night, and two Marines were killed by grenades that landed in their foxholes. The commotion and constant threat of infiltration kept George and most of his company awake, giving them little rest as they waited to be relieved.

10-in-1 rations roll in, as improved beach conditions help the supply lines

The 27th Regiment arrived just as planned at 0800, and Fox Company re-assembled several hundred yards behind the front lines. For most of the men, the only thing that mattered was getting sleep. Captain Caldwell erected his shelter half, recalling "my toes were up in the air." George, likewise, found a hole and quickly fell asleep.

Later that day, Lt. Herbert E. Van Meter, 2/26 chaplain, and several volunteers helped collect the dead Marines, including those who had been hastily buried. It was a gruesome and somber assignment, bringing the regiment's morale to near an all-time low.

By afternoon, George's platoon was issued "10-in-1" rations, offering a full day's meal—breakfast, lunch and dinner—for ten men. Each meal had various canned meats or stews, butter spread, powdered coffee, pudding, jam, evaporated milk, vegetables, biscuits, cereal, beverages, candy, salt, sugar, a can opener, toilet paper, soap, and paper towels.[1] The meals were much better tasting than the K rations, and even the packaging reminded the men of home. Of particular interest were the vegetable cans that bore labels from home rather than the omnipresent olive drab that adorned all things military.

The morale improved even more when a Red Cross representative distributed toiletries, tobacco, and writing materials. With the afternoon sun warming the day, bare-chested Marines hunched over rocks and other makeshift tables, writing letters to loved ones. It was one of the best morale boosters of the campaign.[2]

Marines engrossed in their mail

George was never much of a letter writer, but he decided he had better write home for his parents' sake. As he sat on a rock thinking about what he could write in his letter, he was fully aware that his parents would be worried for his safety, and he was eager to put them at ease. He also knew that he couldn't fool his father by leading him to believe he was not facing any danger. George chose instead to take a humorous approach to his letter. He admitted he had been hit with several tiny grenade fragments in his butt, and that they "stung like crazy." But he reminded his father about his favorite saying of "get the lead out" when his boys were working too slowly. He told his father, "Dad, now you can say it legitimately, because I really do have lead in my butt!"[3]

George removed the bandage from his head and replaced it with a clean dressing. His eye was still swollen, but he could now see out of both eyes. Throughout the day, he continued to pick out shards of metal from his face, legs and buttocks.[4] He was still covered in blood, and his clothes were stiff with sweat, grime, and sand. He wanted to have a shower, but water was still at a premium, especially this close to the front lines.

The occasional mortar round would land near their position, but most of these salvos were ignored. Marines had learned to discern the sound of an incoming round and determine its trajectory. They would take cover only when they suspected it was coming toward them.

Half a helmet of water will go a long way when you have very little

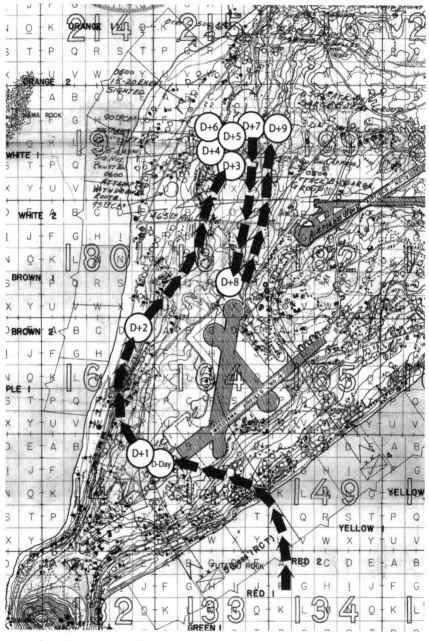

Approximate location of Fox Company on D+9 as indicated on an operations map

CHAPTER SEVENTEEN

D+9: DIG AND HOLD

The men of 2/26 remained in regimental reserve until the afternoon of D+9, February 28th. At 1500 hours, Fox Company was called to reinforce the lines being held by 3/27.[1] George and his platoon moved ahead with Hill 362A looming to the northeast, the highest point on the western side of the island.

3/27 was taking significant casualties from Japanese grenades, among other weapons, in an attempt to control the base of Hill 362A. The hill was pockmarked with a variety of superbly camouflaged pillboxes, dug

Men moving up to the front lines, others returning

out caves and blockhouses. At the top were sheer cliffs, descending 40 to 60 feet below the sharp, jagged edges, with rocks below the cliffs stacked at a steep angle, evidence of recent erosion. This hill was at the core of the Japanese main line of defense on the western side of the island, and they defended it as such.

At 1500 hours, a runner was sent back to retrieve Fox Company and guide them to the front lines. Captain Caldwell led his company as they walked cautiously along a well-worn trail past two known tunnel entrances and near several machine gun nests and artillery emplacements. By dusk, they had advanced beyond the lines established by 3/27. They were approximately 300 yards from the northern beach to their left and about 700 yards due west of Hill 362A.

Each platoon leader gave the order to spread out behind the men of 3/27, who were in the middle of a heated firefight. Quickly, Fox Company ran forward, protected by 3/27 line, and began to "dig and hold."

After several hours, a large number of Marines were heard moving in the darkness, and suddenly Fox Company began taking casualties from grenades and rifle fire. At 0200, Captain Caldwell received reports that 3/27 had abandoned their positions, leaving Fox Company alone on the front line.

Captain Caldwell recalls, "I found out that we were out on the point. We were set up to reinforce 3/27, and I didn't know what to do. There we were, stuck way out there, nobody giving us any word to pullback, so we didn't."[2]

George treated several casualties; most were fragment wounds from grenades, something he was familiar with at this point. As they worked on their fallen comrades, corpsmen were especially vulnerable to grenades as they were often key targets for the Japanese.

John Willis, a corpsman of 3/27, was treating casualties even as a barrage of grenades were thrown at him. To treat one Marine whose legs were dismembered, he had dragged the wounded man to a shell hole. When the first grenade landed in his hole, Willis swept it away. The second grenade landed next to him, and he tossed it away as well. One by one the grenades kept landing, but he quickly cast each one safely away. Sadly, the eighth grenade was timed to explode upon reaching him, and both Willis and his patient died.[3]

At the end of D+9, Fox Company suffered comparatively few casualties. George still struggled with poor vision, since he could hardly see with his right eye. 2/26 was back on the front lines, dug-in, while the rest of the 3rd and 5th Divisions coordinated their assault of Hill 362A.

Otherwise, the day was not particularly noteworthy. For the 5th Division, casualties had exceeded 4,000.[4] For the entire 5th Corp invasion force, the numbers were even more staggering. Notwithstanding the casualty statistics, intelligence reports had indicated that the Americans had finally tipped the balance of power permanently in their favor. Conversely, the Japanese water and supplies were perilously low, and despite their continued will to fight, their physical strength was waning rapidly.[5]

Knowing the outlook of reinforcements was nonexistent, General Kuribayashi had demanded that his staff hold their ground as long as possible, then retreat to prolong the battle. Retreating was unfamiliar to the Japanese army. It was accustomed to attacking at all costs. A retreat, even though it fulfilled tactical objectives, was met with disdain among the common foot soldiers and drained their morale. One Japanese soldier complained in his diary, "We don't fight, we just retreat. The enemy is right before our eyes and we retreat."[6]

The break from the front lines had been dearly welcomed by one and all in Fox Company. They needed the time to rest, eat a good meal, and wash up, so the short break helped revitalize their spirits. But they were far from being able to take a shower, change to clean clothes, or shave. That wouldn't come for weeks. This night Fox Company was again on the front lines—somewhat by accident—and despite the American advances, the enemy was as fierce and determined as ever.

That night, other elements of 2/26 were assigned to set up listening posts along the western beaches, which they accomplished with little resistance. Four posts were established, and each post was assigned a war dog and a handler. Fortunately, the battlefront was quiet, and the only resistance they experienced during the night was insubordination from the dogs, who objected to staying awake.[7]

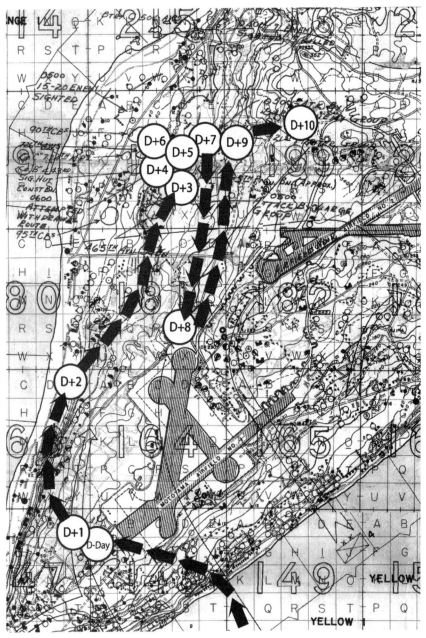

Approximate location of Fox Company on D+10 as indicated on an operations map

Chapter Eighteen

D+10: Taking Hill 362A

After Fox Company learned they were stranded on the front line, they had little option but to settle in for the night. Some men were close enough to the enemy, as they settled into their dug-in positions, that they accidentally crossed paths. Just after 0130 hours, a Japanese soldier was heard rattling a can looking for water. Supply Sergeant John Berg was resting in his foxhole when the small Japanese soldier tripped and fell on top of him. Berg didn't have his weapon close enough to use, so he yelled several expletives at the enemy soldier in his deep, thunderous voice. The small man jumped up and scurried away, leaving his bucket behind. All the Marines within earshot heard the exchange and chuckled because Berg was able to send the enemy soldier packing using nothing more than his voice. They wished all enemy exchanges could be so easy.[1]

At 0215, a Japanese artillery shell scored a direct hit on the 5th Division's ammunition dump. The resulting fire lit up the sky like a fireworks exhibition as artillery and mortar shells flew through the air. The southern end of the island was ablaze with exploding shells as white phosphorus missiles left beautiful arcs across the sky. [2]

Marines scrambled to rescue the ammunition from the fire, ignoring the hailstorm of projectiles swirling about. Some men were burned and others knocked off their feet by exploding shells. The fire raged for hours until fearless Marines manning bulldozers covered the burning boxes with the usually good-for-nothing sand. By 0700 the fire was contained, but the 5th Division had lost a quarter of its ammunition. Amazingly, not one person had died.[3]

5th Division ammunition dump explodes

When Fox Company was escorted to its current position the previous evening, the men traveled under the cover of darkness. The steep, rocky terrain was not what George had expected, and by daybreak, he could finally assess their position. Surveying the terrain, he noticed the superior fighting position of the enemy because each ravine provided excellent camouflage for a Japanese rifleman. The Japanese marksmen remained hidden in their positions, looking over the edge of the ravine. When a Marine came into view, they could easily cut him down. This practice left two or three dead Marines piled on top of each other. According to Captain Caldwell, "These Japanese were having a field day, just sitting there waiting until a Marine came into his view, and he would kill them." When the Japanese army retreated using the miles of honeycombed tunnels, the hidden enemy soldiers were not connected to the extensive tunnel network and were unable to move. These "bypassed" combatants remained in their positions behind the advancing Marines, and simply picked off as many Marines as they could before being killed themselves.

At 0800, 3/27 returned to relieve Fox Company from its positions. One officer stated, "We've passed the crisis, we don't need you anymore." Without any retort, Fox Company gladly marched rearward to reassemble for the next attack. When the men finally stopped walking, they were several hundred yards behind the lines in an area they had fought in several days before.

The day's attack was spearheaded by 2/28, making its first assault since taking Mount Suribachi. Their initial assault of Hill 362A was preceded by the typical artillery barrage. Once on the move, they made rapid progress up the hill, but became stranded on an 80 foot cliff overlooking a rocky slope below. Attempts to free 2/28 were unsuccessful as the entrenched Japanese fought furiously to maintain control of this strategic bastion.

At 1245, orders were received for 2/26 to reassemble in an area just down the ridge from the spot where they had spent the night. After a reconnaissance patrol learned the area was still not secured, the orders were delayed until 1500.[4]

As darkness enveloped the island, the men of Fox Company dug-in about a hundred yards behind lines and were getting buttoned down for the night.

Japanese mortars still pounded away at known Marine positions throughout the night, but mostly the fire was directed at the 1000 yard front line positions being held by the 5th Division.

Several hours after dark, George heard the rustling of many feet stepping heavily on rocks and sand, heading his way. A large number of men came into view in the moonlight. George watched as the line of more than 100 replacements stopped at the Battalion HQ, to be assigned to the various regiments in the battalion. A handful were assigned to Fox Company, and were instructed where to dig-in.

It was obvious to the now battle-hardened Marines of Fox Company that these were "dressed Marines" who had never seen combat. In the morning, the daylight confirmed they were clean shaven, had new boots, and wore clean dungarees.

The new men put on their best act not to appear weak or afraid as the sounds of battle echoed not far in the distance. Several days into the campaign, men from the original landing team had abandoned the charade of never showing fear. All Marines were afraid, and it didn't matter who knew it.[5]

George knew how difficult it would have been had he been a replacement. He sympathized with these men because they were thrust into a combat situ-

Replacements move up to the front

ation, separated from the men with whom they trained. Unfamiliar with the men of this unit, they would undoubtedly feel isolated and vulnerable.

As was common among replacements, their desire to avoid being isolated resulted in their taking unnecessary risks. The overzealous replacements were highly likely to be killed or maimed. Statistically, the casualty rate among replacements was significantly higher than among the battle-experienced troops. Replacements were often casualties on their first day of combat, so Marines didn't want to know much about them. Despite it being unfair to the new men, they didn't want to become emotionally attached, only to watch them be killed.

As the replacements began to settle in for the night, it was equally obvious that the new men required some quick lessons on how to survive on Iwo Jima. When Fox Company regulars heard the thud of a "Burping Bettie" being launched, they scrambled to find cover.

The replacements were bewildered by the strange behavior until they watched the huge 320-mm mortar forge a crater half the size of a tennis court. It took only once for them to learn the sound of the "Burping Bettie," and they understood the need to follow the example of the combat-experienced Marines.

By midnight March 1, Hill 362A, and the ridge leading west to the beach, had been secured at a heavy cost.

Unofficially, Fox Company had suffered 96 casualties. Of the men who originally landed on D-day, 27 had been killed immediately or later died from wounds. Captain Caldwell's company fought at approximately 60 percent of their combat efficiency.[6]

For the Division, an even 1,000 men had been killed, and almost 3,300 were wounded or missing. Within the Division's area of responsibility, Americans could account for 3,252 dead Japanese soldiers, and just twelve prisoners.[7]

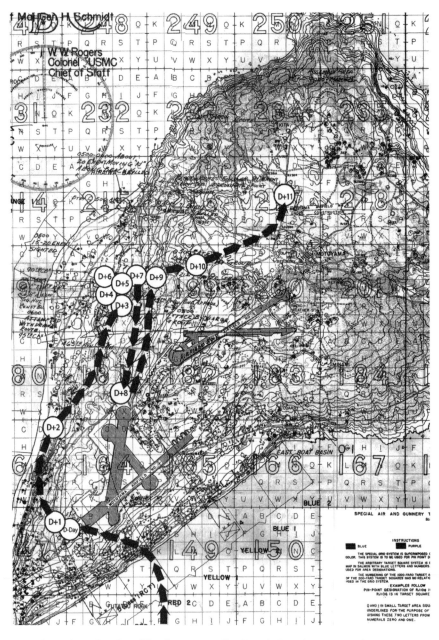

Approximate location of Fox Company on D+11 as indicated on an operations map

General Kuribayashi had given orders for his men to get through the American lines after dark. Kuribayashi had even sent a communication to Tokyo complaining of his lack of success. "The lookout American forces has become very strict, and it is difficult to pass through their guarded lines," Kuribayashi lamented.[1] The Japanese then employed a new tactic, choosing to reserve their forces for the battles yet to come. That night, only a few Japanese patrols succeeded in crossing the American lines, but most of those infiltrations were desperate searches for water.[2] The Marines, stepping up their patrols, were able to locate and kill a significant number of "bypassed" soldiers who were unable to retreat back into the labyrinth of honeycombed tunnels.[3]

George awoke and joined several of his platoon mates as they ate K rations for breakfast. Fox and Dog Companies awaited their jump-off at 0800 hours to support the attack of 3/26.

The 13th Marines were allocated 600 rounds of 105-mm artillery for the day to support the 2nd Battalion.[4] Much of the day's ammunition was spent on the initial barrage before the attack. The Navy's big guns pitched in as well, giving the enemy a taste of the 16-inch guns.[5]

Early that morning, Captain Caldwell was told that Fox Company was needed to fill a gap created by 3/26 and 1/28. Both Fox and Dog Companies broke off their advances to report to duty on 1/28's left flank. As the Fox and Dog Companies disengaged their attack, the retreating Marines were hit with intense sniper fire, causing many casualties. George continued to treat these casualties, and evacuate the wounded men, despite a hail of bullets.

In addition to the sniper fire, minefields were a menace to repositioning men. Throughout the day, engineers were busy clearing the minefields and marking the cleared path with white warning tape. It was a painstaking process, accomplished despite constantly being under fire.

As Fox Company filled the gap created by the steady advances of 3/26, they were forced to advance through another open area marked as a minefield. One by one, each man carefully and deliberately stepped on the white tape as they tried to avoid stepping on a mine.

The concentrated line of Marines offered a tempting target for the Japanese mortarmen. Within minutes, the mortar shells began bursting at the front of the line of Marines. Desperate to avoid the mortars, several men panicked and jumped into the minefield, leaving the safety of the white tape. When a mine exploded, it shot shards of metal flying horizontally toward the legs of Marines who had the presence of mind to stay out of the minefield.

Several men were injured, one losing his legs, another one leg, and the platoon sergeant suffering from facial injuries. According to PFC Rudy Mueller, "I thought he was blinded, the way his face looked, but I found out later he had sight."

George was fortunately far enough away from the attack that he wasn't hurt. By the time he arrived on the scene, corpsmen from other platoons had finished treating the wounded men. Despite the losses, their advance continued amid ongoing mortar and artillery attacks.

As Fox Company progressed northward toward the cliffs, they encountered fewer concrete emplacements. Instead, the island's terrain became the enemy's most effective form of opposition. Rather than facing prepared defensive positions that had thus far dominated the landscape, rocky outcrops and gorges now plagued the Marines' advances. Anti-tank ditches were created to prevent wide scale deployment, and every effort was made by the Marines to fill these gullies. One tank ditch near Nishi ridge was laboriously filled in time for the tanks to help 2/26 in their attack north of Hill 362B. By 1700, the 5th Division had 28 tanks fully engaged, with three tanks modified with flamethrowers.[6]

Continuing their deliberate move up the hill, several Marines were attempting to overtake a gun emplacement when one Marine was hit by a mortar shell. His legs were torn apart, leaving him unable to walk, and he

Group of dead Marines after receiving a direct artillery hit while taking cover in a shell hole

yelled for a corpsman. George quickly crawled on his stomach to help the wounded Marine. The Marine shouted angrily, hammering the ground with his fist because of the unbearable pain. Even though the Marine weighed almost 200 pounds, George, who weighed much less, was determined to get him out of the line of fire. He stood on his feet, bent down to grab the man under his armpits, and with all his effort, dragged him to a safer area. George had moved the Marine several feet when a large shell suddenly exploded just behind them.

The blast hit George with the intensity of a Joe DiMaggio baseball bat swung squarely into his back, and he was sent flying. When he landed on the ground, he was dazed and confused. He remained there for several minutes, unable to move or protect himself. He fought the haze that enveloped his mind, and after a few long minutes slowly came out of his stupor. His first thought was to help the wounded Marine, but fortunately another Marine

*Iwo Jima caves hold sudden death for the unwary,
and this Marine is taking no chances*

was close by and had summoned the stretcher-bearers. Realizing he was
still in the line of fire, George tried to reach forward with his left hand, but
it wouldn't move. His left shoulder and arm rested limply next to his side.
Partially paralyzed, he grabbed a rock with his right hand, and finally lifted
himself to the protection of a shell hole. After ten minutes, he regained his
faculties and was fully coherent. Still partially paralyzed, he began inching
his way down the steep slope to get help with his wound.

George's back was burning with pain, and he was afraid to look at his shoulder because he didn't know if it would be there. Still, he continued to inch
his way down the hill toward a shell hole several yards away. Before he rolled
into the hole, he spotted another Marine inside. He asked him to look at his
back to assess the extent of his injuries.

Thirty minutes had passed since the painful blast, and within that time,
the feeling began to return. George gingerly removed his medical bag from
around his neck, took off his jacket and lifted his shirt over his head. The
Marine carefully helped George lift the shirt as far as it would go to fully
expose the injury. George winced as his clothing brushed against the ex-

Marines advance on cave in an attempt to root out an enemy sniper

posed wound. Not wanting to frighten George, the Marine laughed and said, "Oh, Doc, you're OK. You've just got a big hunk of flesh out of your back." George asked several questions to determine the seriousness of the injury until he was satisfied that he was not injured enough to be evacuated.

He removed a battle dressing from his Unit-3 and gave instructions to the Marine of how to clean and dress the wound properly. George opened a package of sulfanilamide and gave it to the Marine who quickly dusted the wound with a cloud of white powder. George then opened a sterile bandage so the Marine could tape the bandage to George's skin.

When George was satisfied with the Marine's medical handiwork, he rested on his elbows, trying not to let his back touch the ground. It took more than an hour for full feeling to return to his shoulder.

As Fox Company made progress toward Hill 362B, they were again ordered to break off the planned attack to support the right flank of 3/26. As night fell, the gap was finally filled, and George and his Fox Company Marines were far from where they started that day—but they didn't have much to show for their efforts.

Marine throws a hand grenade at Japanese soldiers hiding in a cave

Fox Company was now facing steep cliffs at the north end of a 3rd Japanese airstrip still under construction. The cliffs were pockmarked with caves and windblown vertical crevices that created natural hiding places for the enemy. It seemed like hundreds of them were hidden there, determined not to allow the Marines to capture this strategic hill.

Marine mortar fire bombarded the cliffs to help keep the Japanese soldiers pinned down. At the bottom of the cliffs, Marines lobbed hand grenades into crevasses that were twenty feet above them. Cave by cave, crevasse by crevasse, the Marines routed the enemy from their positions and scaled the steep, craggy cliffs.

Despite the darkness, the Marines climbed the lower cliffs to secure caves that provided the enemy with an easy retreat. Hand grenades were exchanged for hours until finally Fox Company successfully silenced the cliffs, at least for the night. In the morning, fifteen Japanese soldiers were found dead at the base of the cliffs.[7]   •

As they dug-in for the night, two men gladly dug a rifle pit to share with George. They knew he was limited in his movement. George didn't realize that the men in his unit considered him a source of inspiration, but they had watched as he repeatedly exposed himself to furious enemy fire to attend to wounded Marines. Among themselves, they took notice, and a few men remarked about George's astounding ability to ignore his own safety. Strangely he had survived despite the concentration of fire directed at him.

In George's mind, he was just doing his job, but in the minds of his comrades, he was the real deal, genuine to his core. He had no guile or pretense about him, and it seemed he didn't know how to act any other way.

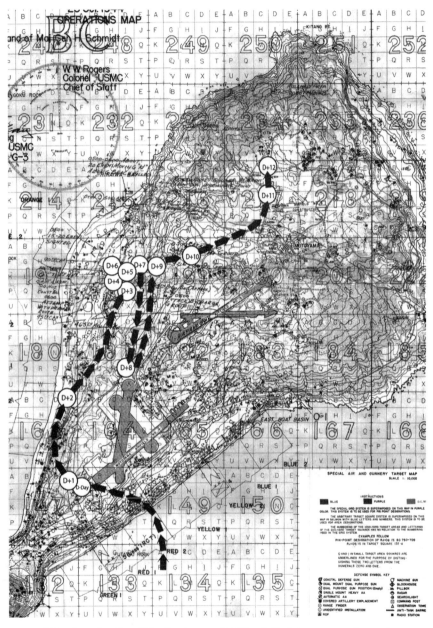

Approximate location of Fox Company on D+12 as indicated on an operations map

George's sore shoulder made it difficult to lie down in the foxhole. He constantly readjusted his shoulders, trying to find the least painful position to rest. That, combined with all the commotion of sporadic enemy mortar and rifle fire continuing to harass their lines, made it difficult to get any rest. Fortunately for the men of 2/26, the Japanese chose not to send infiltrators at them during the night. Instead, forward observers detected the rustling of the enemy busily repositioning troops and equipment. Marine artillery and mortar teams made several attempts with remarkable success to disrupt the enemy's activity. During the night, a total of 45 dead enemy soldiers were found, and a wounded POW was captured and escorted rearward for interrogation and medical care.[1]

During the night, Marine brass finalized their attack plans designed to wrest the high ground of Hill 362B from the enemy's grasp. With Easy and Fox Companies of 2/26 on the right and elements of 3/26 on left, the line of departure created a crescent. Fox Company was assigned to circle around the hill to capture the high ground in front of them. Easy Company would hold their position to the right of them.

At the jump-off at 0745, Marines began their assault, supported by tank fire directed by the battalion command post stationed several hundred yards behind the front lines. Almost immediately, George had to treat men injured by machine gunfire from some amazingly well-camouflaged positions on Hill 362B.

The general consensus among the military planners was to precede an infantry attack with an artillery barrage, since it was believed to be the best way to soften up the enemy. [2] Ask any soldier who has ever survived such an attack, and he would testify to the effectiveness of each blast as the terrific intensity buffets the ground to both deafen and stun the senses with each explosion. But because the Japanese were so well protected underground, some military planners argued that the artillery barrage simply announced to the Japanese that there was impending attack, thus eliminating the element of surprise.

At 0800, the rocket barrage was again used to signal the moment of the infantry attack. Just as the rocket trucks launched their final salvo, Fox Company began to dash down the hill. Their goal was to cross an open valley and engage the enemy near the rocks on the right side. Despite their best intentions, the artillery attack did little to halt the response of the enemy. Instead, the Japanese were waiting for the Americans to cross the open area and reach a point of no return, before beginning their attack.

Quickly, 2/26 moved north and east, taking sporadic sniper and automatic weapons fire. Against the rocks to the right, Sergeant John Danielson led Fox Company's 2nd platoon in their advance against the rocks where the Japanese were cleverly camouflaged. Just as they were fully committed to running through the small valley, the Japanese opened up with machine guns and mortar fire, sending the Marines running for cover.

Dean Keeley and PFC John Repko found shelter in a large shell hole that measured at least ten feet in diameter. It was likely the result of a battleship's 16-inch shell. Twenty or so feet to the right of this large crater, Sergeant Danielson and several other Marines were forced to find protection in the rocks.

A mortar round landed squarely on Sergeant Danielson position. Within seconds another round landed, then another. Dean Keeley and John Repko watched in horror as bone fragments, flesh and whole body parts scattered in every direction. The men were decimated, except one unnamed Marine who was hit in the chest with shrapnel.

Not thinking of the danger, Dean rushed to the scene to find this lone Marine still alive, but bleeding from his mouth. Keeley ripped open his tunic and saw blood oozing from a gaping wound beneath his rib cage. The shrapnel had ripped through the chest wall and punctured a lung. Dean heard the telltale slurping sound coming from the man's chest as the wounded man tried to breathe, indicating a punctured lung.

Remembering his first aid training, Keeley quickly opened up a roll of gauze from his belt. Hoping to fill the hole, he began stuffing the sterile gauze directly into the wound. The Marine was losing a great deal of blood, and Keeley worked feverishly to stop it.

The wounded Marine began to whisper, and as Keeley held the man in his arms he bent down to listen closely to his words. Weak from the loss of blood, the Marine faded in and out of consciousness, but after several slurred words, Keeley realized the man was talking to his mother. Just 18 years old, Keeley was confused about what to do next. He had never held a dying man in his arms.

With tears in his eyes, Keeley talked to the wounded Marine just as he thought his own mother would. Ignoring the din of mortar fire and the chaos happening around them, they spoke tenderly for several minutes before the man stopped whispering and died.

After a long pause, Keeley felt the man go limp in his arms, so he gently let go and laid him down in a shell hole. In an instant, something snapped in his mind. He charged out of the shell hole in a frenzy, pointing his rifle and running directly for the enemy soldiers hiding in the rocks to his right. He stumbled upon a stunned Japanese soldier who was too startled to respond with his weapon. Overcome by rage, Keeley pointed his rifle at the dazed soldier and shot him three times before he hit the ground.

When the soldier hit the ground, Keeley shot him several more times, unable to control the irrepressible fury. Pausing only briefly to look at the dead Japanese soldier, he realized that his rage had compromised his safety. He quickly returned to rejoin his unit. Once he was safe, he was angry with himself for many reasons, but mostly because his fit of rage had exposed him to such danger. Flooded with emotions, he could only cope with them by turning them off in his head. He simply had no choice but to continue fighting.

As had happened five days earlier on D+7, Fox Company was fearless in its attack and gained more yardage faster than any other company on the island.[3] It assaulted the Japanese defenses in terrifyingly close encounters. Despite fierce and desperate clashes, Fox Company ultimately prevailed. Even with the ground gains, George struggled to keep up with the casualties, which happened at an exhausting rate. At times, the wait for stretch-er-bearers seemed to last forever. Just as George finished treating one person, another Marine would call for help. It seemed like an endless effort of crawling from one Marine to the next to treat wounds.

Prevailing against fierce enemy resistance, Fox Company advanced a whopping 300 yards over relatively level terrain by noon. The terrain evolved into deep gorges and large rock formations as they advanced. This slowed down the company, which was now accustomed to making larger gains. Captain Caldwell's men defiantly attacked the enemy positions, sometimes clashing one man against another.

Historically, Fox Company was engaged in one of the most (if not the most) fiercely contested battles of the entire Iwo Jima campaign. It was, without exception, the most successful and deadly assault of the battle.[4] Literally every weapon or implement of war at the Marines' disposal was used to fight this most bitter of fights. By mid-afternoon, Fox Company moved up the hill. Rifle fire was generally useless unless confronted one-on-one with an enemy soldier. Mortars rained down on George's first platoon, and the casualties mounted.

Stretcher-bearers moving across the skyline with empty stretchers for the front lines

*A Marine covers one of the entrances of a Japanese cave, awaiting
the arrival of a flamethrower*

At approximately 1600, a platoon sergeant asked George to go up the hill to find another wounded Marine. Bending down to lower his profile, George crept up the hill, trying to find the man. Several yards away, George shouted down to three Marines who were sharing the protection of a large shell hole and asked if they knew where the man was.

He continued to scramble toward the shell hole, hoping to hear their instructions over the din of battle. Their instructions were interrupted by the sudden deafening explosion of large artillery shell that landed squarely on top of the Marines in the shell hole. George was slammed against the ground, dazed from the blast. George heard the voices of two men screaming in agony as they called for a corpsman. As George lifted himself above the lip of the crater, he was stunned to see the horrifying scene.

One Marine's leg was completely severed, another lost both legs. The last man was obliterated, his human tissue, visceral organs and bone frag-

A rifle indicates another fallen Marine...
It was not uncommon for one foot to cross over the other when rigormortis set in

ments strewn everywhere. George lifted himself up to help the two surviving Marines. But as he stepped on his right leg, he collapsed to the ground as a stabbing pain shot through his leg. He looked down at his foot to see that the inside section of his boot was blown off, leaving his foot and lower leg bleeding.

When he reached down to feel his leg, he knew the bone was broken just above his ankle. He gently peeled away his boot and sock to assess the damage to his foot. He could see that the skin had been peeled away with the blast, but realized the bleeding was not life threatening.

Still determined to do his job, he crawled on his back, pushing with his left leg until he reached the lip of the shell hole. He gently rolled himself down the slope of the hole to reach the two wounded Marines who were both bleeding profusely. He started with the most seriously wounded, wrapping a tourniquet around each leg above the fleshy stumps. Just as he began to

Stretcher-bearers rush a wounded Marine to an aid station

tighten the tourniquet on the second leg, two more corpsmen crawled into the hole with George. They stopped, momentarily daunted by the destruction that single shell had on the group of Marines. George moved to the side to let the uninjured corpsmen finish treating the two wounded Marines.

Since the other corpsmen were busy, he pulled out a battle dressing from his Unit-3 bag, opened a package of sulfanidemide and sprinkled it over his bloody foot. Then he wrapped the battle dressing over his foot and tied it tightly, despite the searing pain. Fearing he would go into shock, he removed a syrette of morphine from his box and stuck the needle in his arm. Within seconds, he could feel the calming effect of the morphine. He also noticed he was breathing at a slower pace. Several minutes later he began to feel calm, but he also had a surge of confidence that he had never previously experienced.

While mortar and artillery shells continued to pound away near his position, George ignored the commotion and watched as the wounded men were carried away on stretchers. The corpsmen told George to stay where he was; they would return to evacuate him as soon as they could. George quietly nodded his head in agreement, acknowledging the inevitability of his evacuation.

As the stretcher-bearers scrambled down the hill toward the aid station, George again heard the cry for "corpsman" up the hill. Realizing that no other corpsman was around, he crawled up to the wounded man to see what he could do to help. George thought that the man was closer than he was; but in fact, the wounded Marine was almost 50 yards away. Ignoring the temptation to turn back, George dragged himself across the rocky terrain that was still taking fire from the hidden Japanese soldiers. As he inched forward, he held his wounded leg off the ground, trying not to bump or drag it.

He could now feel the effects of the morphine making him lose his sense of fear. When he reached the wounded Marine, George could see that both of the man's legs were broken and bleeding. He quickly unwrapped two battle dressings and tied each one firmly around the open wounds. After finishing the job, George administered a shot of morphine because the man was already showing signs of shock. As the medicine coursed through the Marine's veins, he thanked George for crawling up to help him. George said nothing.

With both of them needing further treatment, they realized their chances of being evacuated would improve if they could get closer to a corpsman and further away from the bullets whizzing by. They decided to crawl to a large shell hole down the hill. With the morphine dulling the pain, both men crawled several yards before stopping to rest. They continued inching their way down the hill, finally reaching the relative safety of a large shell hole. It seemed as if they waited for an hour. Finally the stretcher-bearers made it to their position and George watched as his injured Marine friend was loaded on a stretcher. Several minutes later, he too was lifted onto a stretcher and carried rearward.

Halfway to the aid station, as the stretcher-bearers came under sniper fire, they dropped George unceremoniously to the ground as they scrambled for cover. Being left on his own to get out of the line of fire frustrated George, but he couldn't blame the stretcher-bearers for running for cover. The morphine made George feel invincible, so he rolled off his stretcher and reached

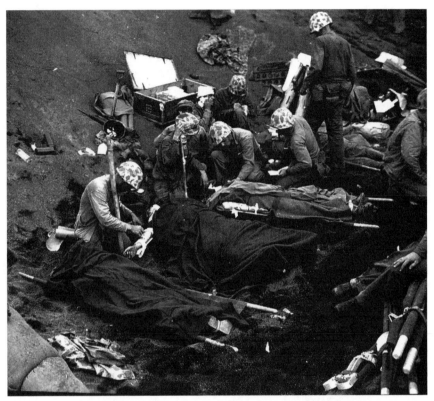

Corpsmen at an aid station work furiously to treat the wounded

for his .45 pistol. He began crawling toward the Japanese emplacement. He had crawled several feet in the direction of the sniper, when the stretcher-bearers returned and dragged him back to the stretcher.

Seeing the stretcher-bearers under fire, two Marines opened fire on the snipers, silencing them within minutes. The aid station was several hundred yards away, which was more than usual, because Fox Company had advanced a record 600 yards that day. When George arrived, he waited several minutes for the corpsman to finish treating the other wounded Marines. He didn't know the corpsman, a replacement who admitted he had landed on the island just a few days before. The corpsman quickly applied a makeshift splint, tightened just below George's knee. George waited for over an hour before being loaded into a waiting truck on which he and three other men were whisked away to the field hospital several miles away.

The driver, having made this trip many times, had learned to drive fast to avoid being a sniper target. George couldn't lie on the stretcher, so he sat up, trying to lift his leg off of it. With each bump and jolt, he felt the grinding sensation of his broken bones rubbing together in excruciating pain. He begged the driver to drive slower, but the man refused and continued his reckless trek on the rough, sandy road.

As the field hospital came into view, the driver finally slowed down to pull up near the tent. George was shocked by the horrible scene. His eyes were drawn first to the dead Marines lined up in a row, draped in green camouflaged ponchos. Rigor mortis had set in on several of these corpses, making their arms and legs difficult to hide underneath the makeshift drape. Outside the tent, a sea of wounded men lay on stretchers waiting anxiously to be seen by a battalion surgeon. Each man wore the stained bandages that reflected an evacuation-worthy injury. Some bore the blood stained dressings around their head, shoulders or legs, while others were missing entire

Marines, covered in their ponchos, lie on the beach they gave their lives to win... A few thousand yards away, the battle was still on

limbs. They slept restlessly, due to the effects of the sedating morphine.

George expended all his remaining energy trying to hold onto his leg, bracing himself through each dip and bump. Several corpsmen came out of a tent to greet the ambulance and helped lift George and the other Marines off the truck. George remained outside, and was told he would wait several hours before the battalion surgeon could see him. He could do nothing but nod his head in acknowledgment.

As he rested on his cot, George began to review the events of the day in his head. He couldn't remember how many men he had treated, but he suspected it was the worst day of their entire campaign. In fact, it was the most costly day for Fox Company and 2/26 in terms of casualties. For Fox Company, only 82 men remained of the original 250 who had landed on the island on D-day. On this day, Fox Company suffered 49 casualties: 19 died, while the other 30 men were evacuated.[5]

From his cot, George could hear the moans of wounded men, and was frustrated that he could do nothing to help them. The darkness was periodically lit by bright flashes, followed by thunderous booms several seconds later. George felt disappointed that he had to be evacuated, and lonely without his Fox Company buddies for the first time in months. His time on Iwo Jima was over; the rest of his Division would take another 23 days of relentless fighting before the island was captured.

T oo tired to think about how long he would wait to see the doctor, George dozed off. An hour later, he woke to see a corpsman holding a bottle of plasma and a large needle.

The corpsman said matter-of-factly, "I need to give you this —doctor's orders."

"I didn't lose much blood. I don't need that," George shot back.

The corpsman insisted, but George didn't give in. "I don't need it, and you go tell the doctor that!"

Frustrated, the corpsman stomped back to the doctor and didn't return.

George spent the next few hours drifting in and out of sleep, keeping an eye on who was next to be seen by the doctor. Early in the morning, a bleary-eyed doctor woke George and asked him how he was doing. George said his leg was broken and he had other wounds on his back and under his eye. The doctor replied quickly, "We'll have you out on a ship in the morning, and they can take care of you out there. We'll get a better splint on you for the trip."

Several minutes later, a corpsman returned and removed the splint below George's knee. He replaced it with a full leg splint. George, now relieved, fell sound asleep.

He woke the next morning as he was carried to a waiting LCVP. This time, the Higgins boat was transporting men away from danger to a troop-transport ship being used to bring wounded men to hospitals in Guam and Saipan. Hospital ships were unable to keep up with the large number of

Casualties are loaded aboard a tractor after first aid and then
transported to hospital ships offshore

casualties on Iwo, and APAs (attack transport ships) were pressed into duty to transport casualties that were not life threatening.

Onboard, George was happy to get out of his fatigues that were now caked in blood and reeking of sweat, mud, and other things he didn't want to think about. He couldn't yet stand to take a shower, but he was happy to get cleaned up, even if it was just a bed bath. He was even more pleased to be served a hot meal, something he hadn't enjoyed for weeks. The food tasted good, mostly because it wasn't a K ration. For the first time since landing on Iwo Jima, George slept peacefully for several hours. While he slept, the ship filled to capacity with injured men and set out toward Guam.

The onboard doctor looked at George's swollen leg, and ordered a corpsman to replace the splint with a cast. A corpsman cleaned George's leg and wrapped a protective layer of cotton gauze just below the knee, leaving the toes exposed. He dipped the roll of plaster-impregnated gauze in warm water and methodically wrapped the lower foot and leg. Once the entire lower leg was completely wrapped, the corpsman gently used both hands to smooth out rough spots. When the cast dried, George began to use crutches, but each time he straightened his leg, he could feel the movement of his broken bones. When he reported the problem to his doctor, the answer was always, "Give it some time. If it doesn't feel better when you get to Guam, tell the doctor."

The pain didn't let up. Each time George moved in his bed or tried to walk on crutches, he continued to feel it. With only a day before landing in Guam, George was eager to get off the ship.

At Guam, George begged the doctor to replace the short cast with a full-leg cast. The doctor agreed to remove the smaller cast, and the next day, George was finally relieved of the pain.

George spent several days in Guam before being told that he was going to Pearl Harbor. The accumulated effects of rest and good food enabled George to get around the hospital corridors. Mastering his maneuvers on crutches, he was quick to move around beds and tables, and the mobility was very therapeutic.

After several days in the Guam hospital, George moved about the ward with relative ease. As he walked the halls, he heard a familiar voice, that of his platoon sergeant, Joe Malone, one of the first casualties George had treated. He had been hit with an artillery or mortar shell and lost his left leg and hand, while also having his face severely injured. Much to George's surprise, Sgt. Malone was healing well and would recover fully. They visited at length, and George returned each day. They spoke candidly about their battle experiences, laughed about good times in Hawaii and Camp Pendleton, but struggled to speak about the loss of so many of their buddies.

One day, Malone had received a letter from a fellow Marine in Fox Company who described George's incredible acts of bravery during the heat of battle. Malone said, "Doc, I understand you did really well there. I appreciate all you've done for me."

George was so surprised by the comment, he repeated it in his head. Who would have written something like that to the sergeant? Puzzled by the compliment, George tried to push it out of his mind.

The day he was to be transferred to Hawaii, he said good-bye to Sgt. Malone and boarded a transport plane destined for Pearl Harbor. George was transferred to the naval hospital for rehabilitation, since his leg was still not healing well.

While at Pearl Harbor, George met another Fox Company Marine whom he had treated on D+3. George had heard the Marine moaning in pain, his intestines were exposed and lying on the ground. He treated the injury by wetting a battle dressing and getting him evacuated. The young man was doing well, walking around the hospital wards with ease. George was surprised to see him, as he had fully expected him to die. They, too, talked at length about the men they knew—those who survived, and those who didn't.

As the days progressed, George was becoming more frustrated that his leg was not healing. The doctor, also puzzled, recommended that George see a specialist on the mainland. George didn't complain; he was ready to go back home.

He again boarded a cargo plane, arrived in California, where he spent two weeks in a Naval hospital in Oakland. He had hoped to have a specialist determine once and for all why his leg wasn't healing. After several tests and numerous examinations, George was transferred to the U.S. Naval Hospital at Santa Margarita Ranch, based at Camp Pendelton. Ironically, George had now come full circle, having traveled from Camp Pendleton to Hawaii, Iwo Jima, Guam, Hawaii, Oakland, and now back to San Diego.

Hoping to get answers to his poor recovery, George was disappointed to learn that his team of physicians was baffled by the slow recovery. After several days of frustrating delays, George was told he would need surgery to help restore the blood-flow to his damaged tissues.

After the surgery, George awoke from the anesthesia in great pain, even though he had a high tolerance for pain. He hoped that when the swelling subsided, so would the pain, but it didn't. The next day, the pain intensified, and George complained to the charge nurse that his cast was too tight. The nurses agreed to inform the physician, but after a day, nothing had changed. George begged the nurses to remove the cast. When George could stand the pain no longer, he demanded to see the doctor to complain about the pain.

The doctor arrived at George's bedside and listened to his plea to remove the cast. The doctor reluctantly agreed. As his cast was cut in half, George could feel the relief of the decreased pressure. Doctors peeled away the protective gauze covering his leg to see that his skin was beginning to turn black. For some reason, the blood flow to his lower leg was cut off, resulting in much of the tissue becoming necrotic. George feared that his leg was gangrenous and would require amputation. He was rushed into surgery as surgeons attempted again to improve the blood-flow. All George could do was hope that his leg did not require amputation.

The next day, he realized he was not feeling the same level of pain as he had experienced after his first surgery. When the doctor examined the leg, he could see it was beginning to heal, but it would be weeks or months to know for sure.

Day after day, his leg continued to improve. Slowly the blackened skin was replaced with pink, healthy skin. After many weeks, George's foot was still not well, but most of the pain had subsided. It would still be months before he could walk on it.

CHAPTER TWENTY-TWO

FROM PATIENT TO "PILL PUSHER"

C amp Pendleton's hospital was dedicated in the fall of 1943 as the U.S. Naval Hospital at Santa Margarita Ranch. This $5 million facility boasted all of the state-of-the-art facilities known at the time, including an "electrically heated food conveyer… [and]… a portable diet kitchen, [that] moved from bed to bed."[1] The hospital was also unique in offering separate quiet rooms designed for "sick officers and critically ill enlisted men."[2] Although quite a few of these quiet rooms existed, most enlisted men convalesced in traditional hospital wards. On each wall of the long, narrow room was a row of freshly painted white hospital beds

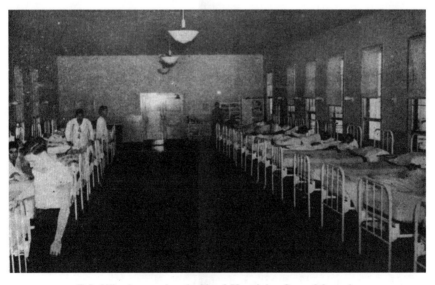

Rehabilitation ward at the Naval Hospital at Santa Margarita
Ranch at Camp Pendleton

with neatly pressed linen. Nurses could easily administer to each patient by simply moving from bed to bed, spaced less than three feet apart.

George settled in to the daily routine at the hospital, but he dreaded the nights because of terrifying nightmares. Night after night, the ghastly scenes of Iwo Jima continued to replay in his mind, especially the shocking scenes of shattered bodies, or the tearful cries of dying Marines. The intensity of his nightmares was a concern to the nursing staff. Patients disturbed by his outbursts during the night complained of the constant commotion in the wee hours of the night. Within days, the doctors ordered George to be moved to a quiet room, in an effort to restore the nighttime peace. His nightmares didn't subside during his entire hospital stay and continued well after his discharge from the service.[3]

George stayed at the U.S. Naval Hospital through April and May to continue his rehabilitation. As his foot still had not healed by the middle of May, the doctors performed a second surgery that had him hobbling around the hospital corridors on crutches for a week thereafter. On George's insistence, the doctors gave him a walking cast, which allowed him the freedom to wander the hospital corridors with relative ease.

Staying day after day in the hospital required finding new ways to pass the time, and he spent many hours talking with other patients. After telling the same stories to the same people, these tales grew more exaggerated as the weeks progressed.

Fortunately, he had other ways of passing the time. After talking about his ability to cut hair and convincing some interested sailors to be his guinea pigs, George approached the hospital barber and asked to borrow a pair of scissors. Instead of lending him a pair, the barber gave him a job. George spent three to four hours a day cutting hair for 25 cents per cut, and became so proficient, $50 was added to his base salary and he was given a percentage of each haircut. As his need for continued rehabilitation lingered from week to week, then month after month, cutting hair was something George anticipated each day. He didn't realize that standing for several hours per day cutting hair may have slowed his recovery.

Out of boredom, he took up smoking cigarettes. The cigarettes were available because Red Cross volunteers gave patients a free pack of cigarettes, and placed them at the foot of their bed each day. For George and many patients there, smoking helped break the monotony.

When he occasionally received a liberty pass, he usually hitchhiked up to Los Angeles to see his Aunt Lillian. His Navy uniform made it easy to hitch a ride, but wearing a walking cast gave him added benefits, as people would go out of their way to drive George directly to his Aunt's house.

During the early summer months, his slow recuperation was a constant source of frustration, and he longed to be anywhere else but in the hospital. He still walked with a noticeable limp, and despite physical therapy, his foot still wasn't healing well.

The first week of August, George was authorized convalescent leave, and he made arrangements to go to his parents home in Utah. After spending nearly two days on the train, he arrived at Ogden's Union Station and was reunited with his parents and family. George was relieved to be home, and during his stay he spent many hours visiting with friends who would come to see him. George didn't want to bring attention to himself by walking with a limp, but the pain still bothered him and he couldn't hide his discomfort. He was also frustrated with not being as mobile as he had hoped.

On August 6, 1945, the news of the atomic bomb having fallen on Hiroshima swept through Northern Utah like a desert grassfire. George, like most Americans, was hopeful that the bomb would lead to the end of the war. When the Japanese didn't immediately surrender, the news of the second bomb dropped on August 9 on Nagasaki elevated hopes of the Japanese capitulation.

Surrender rumors continued for several days in the newspapers and on the radio. Conversations in pubs and barbershops around the country speculated that the end of the war was imminent, and even news reports predicted the inevitable Japanese surrender. But it wasn't until August 14 when President Truman broke the news at a press conference of the Japanese surrender, that the speculation was finally put to rest.

Despite calls for Americans to behave with the appropriate "dignity and solemnity of the occasion," President Truman's official announcement led to pandemonium around the country. One newspaper reported that news of the surrender hit "with the force of Uncle Sam's new atomic bomb and was the signal for everybody to unloose that pent-up feeling, and start— what old-timers view—as the most wild, spontaneous and enthusiastic celebration ever."[4]

In Utah, the news of V-J Day brought spontaneous celebrations as people congregated in city centers statewide. When George heard the news, he hobbled to join a raucous party in downtown Ogden. The drinks flowed freely along the notorious 25th Street, and celebrations continued late into the night.

The Japanese formally surrendered on September 2, 1945, when representatives of the Japanese Empire boarded the USS *Missouri* and signed the official instrument of surrender. Celebrations erupted again when the document was signed. By this time, George had returned to the Naval Hospital and joined the celebrations there.

In early September, George was called into the hospital commander's office. As he walked into the room, several officers and NCO's were there to greet him. He was stunned to learn that they were gathered to honor him for a medal ceremony. He was even more stunned to learn that he was to receive the Navy Cross, and a Gold Star, in lieu of a second Navy Cross, the second highest honor given for heroism in combat. At the ceremony, the commander read the citation explaining why George was being honored. It read :

> *In the name of the President of the United States, the Commanding General, Fleet Marine Force, Pacific, takes pleasure in awarding the Navy Cross to*
>
> *Pharmacist's Mate Second Class, George E. Wahlen, United States Naval Reserve, for service set forth in the following citation:*
>
> *"For extraordinary heroism in action against the enemy on IWO JIMA, VOLCANO ISLANDS, while attached to a Marine rifle company during the period of 19 February to 3 March, 1945. On 26 February, though painfully wounded in the left eye [sic][5], Pharmacist's Mate Second Class WAHLEN remained on the battlefield, and went forward to render first aid to a Marine who was wounded in front of the company's lines, carrying him back to safety through heavy fire. Pharmacist's Mate Second Class WAHLEN then remained on duty with the company through its periods of heaviest fighting, constantly disregarding his own safety in order to render first aid to wounded Marines. Later, Pharmacist's Mate Second Class WAHLEN voluntarily went through heavy mortar fire and rifle fire to give assistance, and worked under continuous fire, treating a total of fourteen men before returning to his platoon. His heroic*

conduct was in keeping with the highest traditions of the United States
Naval Service."

Signed
H.M. Smith
Lieutenant General
U.S. Marine Corps

George recognized the signature, for almost everyone knew General Holland M. Smith, better known as General "Howlin' Mad" Smith, the fiery commander responsible for the Marine's invasion force on Iwo Jima. George was overwhelmed both by the citation and the hearty handshakes from the officers congratulating him. Later that night as he sat on his bunk looking at the citation, he thought, "Wow...two Navy Crosses...is this happening to me?"

When other sailors learned of George's medals, they playfully both teased and congratulated him. Embarrassed by the fuss, he quickly learned to avoid mention of his awards.

Days after receiving his awards, the doctor's assessed George's injured foot again, and determined it was still not healing properly because of poor circulation. George was still suffering a great deal of pain, and walking was very difficult.

Despite their best efforts, Navy physicians met with him again to reveal that a third operation was needed. Hearing the news, George was angry and frustrated. He was irritated that his foot was taking so long to heal, because he longed to be with his unit. Although George didn't want to see combat again, he desperately wanted to be with his comrades.

The third surgery was finally successful in forcing blood to circulate at the point of his fracture. George again spent several days on crutches before he was given a walking cast. After months of waiting, he was beginning to feel less pain, and he allowed himself to hope that his foot would actually heal. Up until this point, he believed that he would always walk with a limp.

Months after peace was declared, war bond drives were still actively trying to raise funds through various patriotic events, and often featured recently decorated veterans to help make the pitch. In late September, George received a telegram notifying him that he was being ordered to report to the Naval Barracks in Washington, DC at 8:30 a.m. on October 3, 1945. Without other explanation, he supposed that with his two Navy Crosses, he was being pressed into duty as a pitchman for the "Mighty 7th War Bond Drive."

George arrived at the New York airport on Monday, October 1, and hopped a train to Washington, DC. He had arrived two days before he was ordered to arrive for duty, so he checked into a hotel and ventured out to see the sights. On Wednesday, October 3, George reported for duty at 8:30 a.m. and was immediately accosted by a Navy officer, who demanded, "Where have you been? We've been looking all over for you."

George promptly pulled out his orders and reminded the officer that he wasn't scheduled to report for duty until that very moment. The officer, flustered, could only reply, "Don't you know why you're here?"

George replied courteously, "I'm not sure."

Dumbfounded, the officer stared at George and said, "On Friday, you have an appointment at the White House. You're going to receive the Medal of Honor."

George was speechless. He stood in front of the officer, slack jawed, not responding for several seconds. Finally he smiled shyly, looked at the officer, and said, "No kidding?" The officer smiled, shook George's hand, and was the first to congratulate him.

October 5, 1945 was Nimitz Day in the nation's capitol, a day to honor Fleet Admiral Chester W. Nimitz, and his successes in directing the Pacific Fleet during the war. George was one of 14 men to receive the Medal of Honor, including eleven Marines and two others from the Navy.

George checked into the Statler Hotel in downtown Washington. Friday morning, he waited in a crowded hotel lobby for the official car to take him to the White House. Out of nowhere, George heard a familiar voice yelling, "Doc!" and he strained his neck to find the source. Suddenly, Marine Private Franklin E. Sigler grabbed George's hand. They were both members of Fox Company, had landed on Iwo Jima on February 19, and both were to be recipients of the Medal of Honor. They had last seen each other eight months earlier in the shadow of Mount Suribachi when Sigler received a minor wound that George had quickly treated.

Private Sigler was recognized for single-handedly eliminating a gun emplacement, charging up a hill and eliminating more enemy combatants. Although injured in the skirmish, he refused to be evacuated, and even carried three platoon-mates to safety.

For the few minutes they had before leaving, they quickly reviewed the last eight months, and George enjoyed the comfort of having a familiar face to talk to.

When George arrived at the White House he was terrified to see all the dignitaries and officers. George had rarely interacted with officers ranked above a captain. He was dumbstruck to learn that the onlookers included Generals George Marshall, George Patton, and Hap Arnold, Admiral Nimitz, and Secretary of Defense James Forrestal.

Private Franklin E. Sigler, also a Medal of Honor recipient from Fox Company, 2/26

George sat nervously in his chair, sitting next to the other medal recipients. After the bands played and the dignitaries made their speeches, they began calling each recipient alphabetically to receive his medal from the President.

Upon hearing his name, George walked tentatively across the portico to salute the Commander in Chief. He was so terribly nervous that he stopped several feet in front of President Truman. Seeing George's nervousness, the president reached out his hand for George's. Not noticing the president's outstretched hand, George could only stand anxiously at attention while looking at the ground. After a brief pause, President Truman reached again and latched on to George's hand to draw him closer. He then whispered in George's ear, "It's mighty good to see a pill pusher here in the middle of all these Marines." Although George was trying to keep his composure, he couldn't help but smile at the President's remarks.

After presenting the Medal of Honor to George,
President Harry S Truman extends a hand of congratulations

Both George and President Truman stood at attention while they listened as George's official citation was read to the large crowd.

The President of the United States in the name of The Congress takes pleasure in presenting the Medal of Honor to

GEORGE EDWARD WAHLEN,

Pharmacist's Mate Second Class, for conspicuous gallantry and intrepidity at the risk of his life above and beyond the call of duty while serving with the 2nd Battalion, 26th Marines, 5th Marine Division, during action against enemy Japanese forces on Iwo Jima in the Volcano group on 3 March 1945.

Painfully wounded in the bitter action on 26 February, Wahlen remained on the battlefield, advancing well forward of the frontlines to aid a wounded marine and carrying him back to safety despite a terrific concentration of fire. Tireless in his ministrations, he consistently disregarded all danger to attend his fighting comrades as they fell under the devastating rain of shrapnel and bullets, and rendered prompt assistance to various elements of his combat group as required. When an adjacent platoon suffered heavy casualties, he defied the continuous pounding of heavy mortars and deadly fire of enemy rifles to care for the wounded, working rapidly in an area swept by constant fire and treating 14 casualties before returning to his own platoon. Wounded again on 2 March, he gallantly refused evacuation, moving out with his company the following day in a furious assault across 600 yards of open terrain and repeatedly rendering medical aid while exposed to the blasting fury of powerful Japanese guns. Stouthearted and indomitable, he persevered in his determined efforts as his unit waged fierce battle and, unable to walk after sustaining a third agonizing wound, resolutely crawled 50 yards to administer first aid to still another fallen fighter. By his dauntless fortitude and valor, Wahlen served as a constant inspiration and contributed vitally to the high morale of his company during critical phases of this strategically important engagement. His heroic spirit of self-sacrifice in the face of overwhelming enemy fire upheld the highest traditions of the U.S. Naval Service.

After the citation was read, the President smiled at George and said, "I feel honored to be able to give you the Medal of Honor." He reached around George's head to fasten the clasp around his neck, connecting the blue ribbons that held the dangling star-shaped medal.

George politely replied, "Thank you, Mr. President." He eagerly walked off the portico as the audience clapped enthusiastically. George, happy to be out of the spotlight, dashed back to his seat with the other recipients.

After the medal ceremony, George and the other recipients met with reporters to discuss their new medals. Shortly thereafter, they were whisked away by officials into waiting convertibles. These cars formed a line behind Admiral Nimitz's car, which led a full-blown military parade down Pennsylvania Avenue, complete with marching bands and cheering well-wishers.

After the parade, their motorcade stopped at the U.S. Capitol where they were escorted into the building to be officially presented before a joint session of the U.S. Congress. The festivities continued into the evening, ending with a special banquet. George was introduced to Admiral Nimitz, and they spoke briefly. When George asked for an autograph from the Admiral, he graciously agreed. It was the end of an historic day. George was exhausted. As he reviewed the day's events in his head, he could only shake his head in disbelief.

Chapter Twenty-Three

Home and Discharge

On his trip back to Camp Pendleton, George returned to Ogden with his family and enjoyed several days at home. The local newspaper, the *Ogden Standard-Examiner*, featured his picture and a story with the headline "Utah Sailor Receives Nation's Top Award." The article, written by an Associated Press reporter, read:

"Pharmacists Mate George Edward Wahlen, 21, of Ogden, will never forget the White House ceremony Friday in which he was presented the Congressional Medal of Honor.

He was only one of 14 heroes given the nation's highest award in a mass presentation. But as he stepped before President Truman on the White House lawn he got some special attention.

It had nothing to do with the fact that his citation carried a glowing account of how he had time and again risked his life on Iwo Jima last March to give relief to wounded veterans. What marked him out was the act that he was not a combat man like others.

The 21-year-old Utah boy appeared a little shy and stopped a couple of feet from the president. Surrounding them were high-ranking army and navy officers and cabinet members. Promptly the president reached out a friendly hand, drew Wahlen closer to him and whispered in his ear. The young hero smiled and was much more at ease then as his citation was read." [1]

The day after the newspaper article appeared, George's parents received a call from Ogden City Mayor Kent Bramwell, who wanted George to headline a parade down Washington Boulevard. Terrified of having so much attention, George politely declined the offer by having his parents tell the mayor his injured foot was still bothering him. They said he wanted to return to the Naval Hospital for continued treatment. The next day, he boarded a military plane at Hill Field that took him to the safety of his hospital bed in Southern California.

After arriving at Camp Pendleton, he recuperated from his long journey by staying off his foot. With a few days of rest, his foot was feeling much better. By the first of November, he was hearing rumblings from the doctors that he might be discharged. The week before Thanksgiving he learned he was ordered to report to Camp Shoemaker, near San Francisco, where he would be discharged from the Navy.

He arrived at Camp Shoemaker on November 30, but was disappointed, because his discharge was delayed for several weeks. George was eager to make it home for Christmas, but as each day passed, he was giving up the hope of being home in time. Happily, on December 19, 1945, he learned that his discharge was approved, and he quickly obtained the necessary papers, signed for his final payment, and bought the first available train ticket to Ogden. He was welcomed home on December 21, just in time for Christmas.

He returned to the same small house he had left over two years ago. His return meant that he and his twin brothers would be forced to take turns sharing a bed. The first few nights at home, George woke

Everett B. Kellogg of South Lancaster, Mass.

up his family with terrifying screams from nightmares. As George relaxed into the peace of civilian life, he was unaware of the emotional trauma still flooding his subconscious. All of the horrible experiences continued to replay each night, as his ability to cope with the flood of awful memories was diminished by the rigors of the day's events. When George awoke one night hitting his younger brother sleeping next to him, he was never asked to share a bed with his brothers again.

A week after returning home, George heard a knock on his door, and to his surprise, there stood his senior corpsman from Iwo Jima, Pharmacist Mate 1st Class, Everett B. Kellogg. He was on his way home to South Lancaster, Massachusetts, but his train was delayed in Ogden. Having several hours, Kellogg braved the bitter cold to find George. Knowing of George's notoriety, Kellogg called a reporter from the *Ogden Standard-Examiner* in hopes of finding him. The reporter located George's address and drove Kellogg several miles through the grass-less farmlands west of Ogden. The two friends visited for several hours before Kellogg returned to the train station for his trip home.

Weeks after the holidays, fellow corpsman Bob DeGeus similarly was delayed at Ogden's Union Station, and he too wanted to visit with George. Choosing to miss his train rather than skip this opportunity to see his friend, DeGeus watched his train leave the station before he braved the snow-blown streets of Ogden to find a hotel room.

Choosing one of many seedy hotels on 25th street, he checked into the closest place, telling the clerk he was looking for George Wahlen. The next morning, the clerk located an aunt, who knew that George's father was working just three blocks from the hotel. DeGeus walked the few blocks to the rail yards and asked several employees for help in finding Mr. Wahlen. Several minutes later, DeGeus found George's father sweeping grain out of a boxcar, and he introduced himself. Mr. Wahlen jumped out of the car and shook his hand, and they talked for several minutes. He offered to take DeGeus to see George, and they both climbed into a worn-out Model "A" pickup truck. They rumbled across the bumpy road to the farm west of Ogden. George's father dropped DeGeus off and returned to work. George's mother invited DeGeus to stay and visit as long as he wished. For three days, they laughed, reminisced about good times, and talked openly of the friends they had lost.

In 1946, George, Bob, Everett, and every other twenty-something war veteran were referred to as "boys." Prayers were offered on behalf of the "soldier boys," newspapers announced headlines of this army "boy" who was promoted, or that navy "boy" who was killed or missing in action. For George, and all other returning veterans, these young men had been tempered by life-changing events, and they possessed a maturity well beyond their years. They had earned the right to be called men.

Nightmares continued to plague George at night. His violent, unconscious outbursts disturbed his younger brothers, where the three of them still shared an attic bedroom. Many nights he would call out in the night, and they would protect him from hurting himself during these episodes. Even though George was embarrassed by his nightmares, the issue wasn't discussed among them.

George was eager to find a job, but with so many young men returning from the war, jobs were scarce. Despite being a national hero, George rarely discussed his Medal of Honor, even if it would have helped him get a job.

After several months of looking, he was offered a job as a truck driver for the California Packing Company in Ogden. He was happy to be—at long last—gainfully employed, and he enjoyed the newfound freedom that a paycheck offered. He welcomed having cash in his wallet, if for no other reason than it allowed him to date more often.

His Uncle Lee Lythgoe arranged for George to meet Melba Holley, a beautiful blonde with a radiant smile and a fun-loving demeanor. She lived in Slaterville, a rural farming community west of Ogden. Their first encounter was on a blind date, and George was eager to see her again.

On their next date, George met Melba's father, John A. Holley, who was dubious about his young daughter dating a veteran. John, a veteran of World War I, had learned enough about veterans not to trust them. Also a devout Mormon, he strongly protested George's cigarette habit, which contradicted the faith's religious tenets. As the relationship blossomed, George would

Melba Holley

come to pick up Melba for a date each night. And each night, George listened to Mr. Holley's extended sermons on the virtues of clean living, and the importance of avoiding alcohol and tobacco.

George was not dissuaded by the lectures, and their dating increasingly focused on a long-term relationship. In early June, George proposed to Melba, and she agreed to marry him. But she was only 17 years old, and the state required the permission of her father in order to obtain a marriage license. He flatly refused to sign the papers, later admitting that he had hoped George would give up and go away. With her 18th birthday still eight months away, George said resolutely to Mr. Holley, "I'll date her until she's 18, and we'll get married then!" By July, Mr. Holley could see that George was in it for keeps, and he agreed to permit their marriage. They were married on August 16, 1946.

Before they were married, George was concerned about his ongoing nightmares, and even warned Melba about his often violent outbursts during the night. She was anxiously prepared for the worst. Strangely, the night George and Melba were married the nightmares stopped, and he hasn't been bothered with them since.

The newlyweds lived meagerly on George's wages at the California Packing Company, and it was evident that if they were to survive, George would need a formal education. He used his G.I. benefits to enroll at Weber College in fall quarter 1946. The young couple struggled financially to make ends meet while he attended school, and to complicate matters, their first child, Jolene, was born on December 26, 1947.

During his schooling, he was asked several times to speak before church and civic groups, but it was a task he strongly disliked. He was especially uncomfortable speaking in public, and eventually he declined the speaking invitations whenever he could. Still, the requests continued, and he did what he could, despite growing weary of the demands for his time.

By the end of summer 1948, he had earned a two-year business degree, and shortly after graduating from Weber College, he was hired by the Railway Mail Service to be a mail handler. It was a demanding job, requiring him to work 12 hours per day, seven days a week. Making $1.39 per hour, George now had more money than he had ever known. He thought he could work there temporarily to earn enough money to attend the University of Utah, but the long hours were making him miserable, and his resolve to get his bachelor's degree began to wane.

At a party, he met Arthur Howell, a sergeant in the Army Air Force recruiting office in Ogden. Month after month he encouraged George to quit the job that was making him miserable, and enlist in the Army instead.

Joining the Army solved several problems. First, he could quit his job; second, the government would pay for his education; finally, he could avoid the numerous requests to appear in public. He continued to be asked to speak before groups and organizations, but he never grew comfortable in that role. By joining the Army, he could enjoy the relative anonymity of military life.

He joined the Army on November 28, 1948, and was stationed in Ogden as a recruiter in the Ogden Army and Air Force Recruiting Office. It was a job that required him to get out in the community and meet people, and he became a salesman for the Army. The job was difficult for George initially, because he didn't have an outgoing, gregarious personality. He struggled for several months, performing well below his quota and wondering if he had done the right thing by rejoining the military. A commanding officer took him aside one day and said, "George, I'll make you a deal. You go out and see four people every day. If you see four people by two p.m., take the rest of the afternoon off. But if you won't quit until you've seen four people, I promise you'll be successful."

Taking the advice to heart, George began seeing four people each day. After a month, he was the top recruiter in his district. At a regional meeting of recruiters, the colonel in charge asked George to stand before the large gathering and tell them how he became the top recruiter. George divulged his secret of seeing a minimum of four people each day. He also learned from this experience how self-discipline factors into being successful.

In March of 1950, George and Melba's second daughter Christine was born, and several months later, George learned that he was being transferred to Fort Hauchuca, Arizona. He and his young family moved to Arizona during the summer of 1951. This Army post was closed after WWII, but George's job was to work in the dispensary, and help get it organized, to ensure that it was functioning properly, and efficiently.

George Wahlen in 1949

In 1952, the Korean War dominated the headlines, and George received orders to be transferred to Korea, unaccompanied by his wife and family. It was a difficult assignment, as he had not yet been separated from his family during his tenure in the Army. Like most military families when the husband is sent overseas, the wife must bear the brunt of managing the family, and the Wahlens were no different. Melba was forced to care for their two young children alone, while George completed his tour of duty.

When he arrived in Tokyo for processing, his orders were changed, and he was assigned to stay in Japan at the dispensary at Tokyo General Hospital. He was the chief enlisted NCO in the dispensary, and had increasing responsibilities for managing the operations of the facility. Fortunately, the change of assignment permitted his family to join him in Japan, and George eagerly informed his wife of the news. But it took several months before all the arrangements could be made for her to travel to Japan.

In May of 1952, George and three other enlisted men from the base, driving through Tokyo, were caught up in the May Day Riots. The anti-American sentiment had boiled over, and many U.S. servicemen were assaulted. The rioters, noticing the American car with George and the other servicemen, attempted to overturn their car. George was carrying a .45 pistol, and while the rioters were banging on the car, yelling "Yankee go home," he quietly hid the gun under the car seat. One man in the car looked puzzled and asked George "Why are you putting that away? You may end up using it." George replied confidently, "I don't want to entice them to do any more," so he quietly pushed it under the driver's seat. He instructed the driver to just continue driving, and eventually they drove away from the wild mob.

After almost a year, his wife Melba and their two daughters were finally able to join him in Japan. The voyage lasted several weeks and became even more miserable when the two girls were stricken with chicken pox. They were quarantined in their rooms for most of the trip, even unable to get off the ship when they arrived, as health officials were fearful of spreading the disease on base. George found the officer in charge, and after several tense hours, was finally granted permission to take his family to their apartment off base. Had on-base housing been available, they might have spent several more days on board before being allowed off the ship.

George and his family lived in a small, Quonset-hut type apartment in the Japanese community. They survived the cramped, uncomfortable quarters for three months until government quarters were available on base.

George and his family lived in Japan until August of 1954, when he was transferred to the post hospital in Fort Ord, California. They were happy to return to the States and live closer to their families in Utah.

As a master sergeant (E-7), George held increasingly responsible positions. At his new assignment, he was the personnel sergeant responsible for managing the hospital's enlisted personnel. His office consisted of four enlisted and one civilian employee, but he had never been trained for this job. After a year of asking questions from experienced personnel directors, and making many mistakes, he began to feel comfortable in his position.

While living at Fort Ord, his family nearly doubled in size. In February of 1956, Melba gave birth to their third child, Pam, and in January of 1958, their first son, Blake, was born.

As he neared the end of his assignment at Fort Ord, his commander had recommended that George be promoted to the next pay-grade (E-8). The promotion was disapproved because he only had 13 years of service, instead of the required 15 years. He was 34 years old, too old to be commissioned a 2nd Lieutenant. However, two officers had recognized George's abilities and recommended that he apply for a direct commission as a 1st Lieutenant. The paperwork sat on his desk for several weeks, until one of the officers called from Washington, DC to inquire of the status of the application.

"Well," George replied somewhat embarrassed, "it's still here in my desk."

The frustrated officer instructed George, "You've still got a chance to get your commission, but you'll have to complete the paperwork today and get it up to the 6th Army Headquarters by the end of the day."

6th Army Headquarters was over 50 miles away from Fort Ord, but George hurriedly completed the paperwork and submitted it to the appropriate officers for their endorsement. On July 15, 1959, just ten days after submitting the paperwork, George was officially notified that he was commissioned a 1st Lieutenant.

After George received his commission, he was transferred to Fort Sam Houston, in Texas to attend 12 weeks of Medical Service Corps basic officer training. Upon completion of that course, he was transferred to the Missile Command at Fort Carson, Colorado, and became an assistant S-4 and medical advisor of an artillery group.

During their stay in Colorado, George and Melba bought their first home in Security. It was a big step for them, as they wanted to plan for their future, but the transient military life made buying a home very hard. Fortunately, their decision to become homeowners was a good one, and they were able to rent their home for several years after leaving Colorado.

George was transferred to Korea in February of 1963, and his family moved back to Ogden while he was there. He was assigned to the 168th Medical Battalion as adjutant and personnel officer. He had been in Korea for only a month when he was invited by President Kennedy to attend a special event at the White House Rose Garden for all living Medal of Honor recipients. The event offered him a welcome opportunity to see his family and get a break from his long stay in Korea. His commanding officer attempted to dissuade George from attending the event, but George countered with the argument "How could I say 'no' to our commander in chief?" The officer didn't reply.

George flew back to Utah to briefly see his family before he and Melba flew on to Washington, DC for the event. This visit home was his only leave during his 15-month tour in Korea.

Upon completion of his assignment in Korea, George was transferred to

President John F. Kennedy greets George at a special reception at the White House in February, 1963

the 25th Infantry Division at Schoefield Barracks in Hawaii in June 1964. He came home from Korea and met his wife and family in Ogden before driving to Oakland, California, to board a ship for Hawaii. He was assigned as the administrative assistant to the surgeon of the 25th Infantry Division for the next year.

When his C.O. learned that George didn't have a bachelors degree, he was assigned to the Church College of Hawaii (BYU-Hawaii) for eight months to complete the degree, graduating magna cum laude. Shortly after graduating, George was assigned as the personnel officer at Tripler General Hospital in Hawaii, and during that year-long assignment, he was promoted to the rank of major.

In 1967, President Johnson was committing more troops to Vietnam, and George was notified of his impending transfer there. His assignment to Vietnam was very difficult, especially for Melba. Just before George left for Vietnam, they learned that Melba was pregnant with their fifth child. At age 39, she was left alone to care for their three children: ten-year-old son Blake, and two teenage daughters, Christine and Pam. To add to the stress, their oldest daughter Jolene had just become engaged to be married. With nothing either of them could do to change his orders, George left for Vietnam, hoping all would be well. Weeks after he had left, Melba moved the family off base, where they waited for George to finish his year-long tour.

He was stationed in Long Bin, just outside Saigon, as the assistant personnel officer to the Surgeon's Office, responsible for making all the assignments for the medical service corps officers and assigning all other medical department officers in Vietnam.

It was during this time in Vietnam that George had many long hours to think about his wife and family. During his assignment at Fort Ord, George chose to become increasingly involved in The Church of Jesus Christ of Latter-day Saints (Mormons) and he had enjoyed attending church services and being involved in other activities. However, George continued to smoke, which limited his involvement in his church, because tobacco use was forbidden. Throughout the years, Melba had scolded George for smoking, and despite his countless attempts to quit, he simply couldn't beat the habit. Although he willfully fulfilled church assignments, George's desire for increased spiritual connection with the church was being hampered by his cigarette habit. After being away from his wife and family, he committed to himself to quitting smoking. He recalled, "I didn't have my wife or family asking me to quit, but I just decided to quit on my own. Once I got that commitment in my head, I just quit, and I never wanted to smoke after that."

In late January 1968, he endured the Tet offensive when most American bases were attacked by the Viet Cong. For several days, all the U.S. airfields were closed, and U.S. forces were unable to evacuate the wounded. The hospitals became overcrowded during this extended battle. George spent long nights sleeping in bunkers. After 13 days, the Americans successfully repelled the enemy forces, but ironically, the enemy's offensive galvanized opposition to the war among civilians in the U.S.

In May of 1968, his Vietnam tour was complete, and he prepared to return to his family in Hawaii. After boarding the plane to go home, the flight was delayed several hours because enemy forces had infiltrated near the end of the runway. Marines were called in to clear the area. George endured many tense moments, until he let out a small cheer as he cleared

Vietnam airspace and headed for his family in Hawaii. When he landed in Honolulu, he saw his son Brock for the first time, and they enjoyed a short but well-deserved vacation.

Not long afterwards, they packed up their belongings and began the process of starting a new home at a new location. They boarded ship for the mainland and headed for their new post at Fort Huachuca, Arizona. He and his family lived on base there, and George completed his military assignment as the adjutant and personnel officer at a new hospital on base. He retired from military life on August 11, 1969.

After 18 years away from home, they returned to Utah, where they bought a home in Roy. George was 45 years old when he retired from the Army, and was ready to venture into the unknown world of civilian life. Not knowing what he could do for a living, he worked for 18 months at New York Life as an insurance salesman. Tiring quickly of that line of work, he accepted a position with the Utah State Tax Commission. This job was also short-lived, as George was offered a position with the Veterans Administration. He found

Wahlen family upon arrival in Hawaii, 1964 (left to right) Jolene, Christine, George, Melba (below) Blake, Pam (youngest son Brock born in 1968)

a home at the V.A., where he was employed for the next 14 years.

His years of serving in the Navy, as well as his career in the Army, helped qualify him for early retirement. At age 59, George retired in 1983.

Of course, retirement didn't mean that George stopped working. He became involved with the Utah Military and Veterans Affairs Committee (UMVAC), which was active in advocating veteran's issues.

For the first time, George began to use his status as a Medal of Honor recipient to gain access to influential people. He was amazed to learn how easy it was to get people to listen to him. Initially, UMVAC focused on establishing a state veteran's cemetery, and he worked hard to lobby state legislators for the cause. With George's help, Speaker of the House Nolan Karras agreed to sponsor a bill. The bill passed, and a large tract of land near Camp Williams was selected as the ideal location for the cemetery. Construction began in late 1996, and it was dedicated a year later.

He then focused his attention on the construction of a state-funded veteran's nursing facility. Having worked previously with Senator Orrin Hatch, he enlisted his help in finding the land to build the nursing home. With the

Main entrance to the George E. Wahlen Department
of Veterans Affairs Medical Center

George's efforts and those of many other interested parties, the facility was built in 1998.

On December 6, 2003, President George W. Bush signed legislation authorizing the Salt Lake City Veterans Affairs Medical Center to be named in George's honor. Senator Robert Bennett sponsored the legislation to name the facility the "George E. Wahlen Department of Veterans Affairs Medical Center." On November 10, 2004, local and national dignitaries dedicated the facility at a ceremony that featured speeches by Senators Hatch and Bennett, and other government officials. President George W. Bush wrote a letter endorsing the naming of the facility and congratulated George for his many years of dedicated service.

Epilogue:

From Mettle to Medal

George Wahlen went from a small town farm boy to a decorated American war hero before the age of 21. Since that brisk October morning in 1945 when President Harry S Truman fastened the Medal of Honor around his neck, he has lived as a quiet hero. He rarely discusses his Iwo Jima experiences with anyone, other than the closed brotherhood of veterans who didn't need adjectives to explain what happened there.

George's actions were definitively heroic. He not only witnessed his best friend's final conscious moments, but had he chosen to spend more time trying to save him, others may well have died. Instead, he continued to perform his life-saving duties, pausing neither to consider his own desires or to safeguard himself from mortal danger.

On the battlefield, many of his comrades commented that George demonstrated superhuman strength, carrying men on his shoulders that were almost twice his size. He endured significant wounds to his face, eye and back (accounting for two of his three Purple Hearts), and endured stinging hand-grenade shrapnel embedded in his back and buttocks. (Over the past 60 years he has continued to pick out shards of metal that have worked their way to the surface of his skin.) His third debilitating wound to his foot not only took several surgeries to repair and months to heal, but he has always endured pain in his lower leg. Upon returning from the battle, he struggled with the overwhelming emotional pain caused from witnessing so many traumatic events.

He has always been surprised by the attention he receives for simply doing what he was trained to do. He has never considered himself brave, gallant, or intrepid, though he saw such characteristics in the Marines and fellow corpsmen he grew to love and respect.

After he married, George didn't talk to his wife about his war experience, or the medals he had earned during the war. She didn't know about his Medal of Honor until many years after they were married. Neither did his children know their father was a national hero until most of them were teenagers. They had rarely discussed his war experiences, and it wasn't until Weber State University awarded him a lifetime achievement award and produced a video profile of his life that they were aware of the extent of his heroism.

Certainly he had many opportunities to leverage his medal status into special benefits or privileges, but all evidence indicates that he did just the opposite. He left his medals at his parents' house; his mother safeguarded them for many years after the war. And despite the numerous invitations to speak at various civic events and functions, he managed to minimize the significance of the award to his wife, and downplay national notoriety he had achieved. It wasn't until he received an invitation to attend the inauguration of Dwight D. Eisenhower in 1952 that she began to comprehend the significance of his being a Medal of Honor recipient. Indeed, George has always been a reluctant hero, and has learned to endure the adulation and public honors by reasoning that he stands as a proxy for all of his fellow veterans.

George is the quintessential American veteran, having served tours of duty in World War II, Korea, and Vietnam. He served in almost every branch of the service, working as an aircraft mechanic for the Army Air Corps, being inducted into the Navy, volunteering for the Marines, and enlisting in and retiring from the Army. His life has been an example of love for his country, dedication to his family, and service to God.

To this day, a week doesn't go by that George doesn't receive a request in the mail for his autograph. He dutifully signs his name as requested, and often pays for the return postage when a child forgets to include it.

Through all of his life, George has remained true to his indomitable character. As he had done many times in his life, he found a way to do what he thought was right. Even today, he doesn't consider what he did as a corpsman heroic, although he knows it has been called such. They were extraordinary times, filled with extraordinary people.

For George Wahlen, he feels lucky to have done his part and performed his duty in bitter circumstances. He sees himself as but one of thousands, both the living and the dead, who defended their country with honor on the volcanic sands of Iwo Jima.

George Wahlen was evacuated from Iwo Jima on March 3, 1945, but the battle continued for another 24 days. Of the 250 original men of Fox Company who landed on the island, only a handful walked off the island. Captain Caldwell was among the very few company-level commanding officers that wasn't a casualty.

When the island was declared secure, the remaining Marines left the island on March 27, 1945 for the 17-day journey back to Hawaii. The time aboard their troop transports ship was spent reflecting on the events on the island. Captain Caldwell spent much of his time writing letters to the 67 families of the men in his company who died. It was the highest casualty rate of any company in the Marines during any single operation of the war.

When they returned to Hawaii, they went to Camp Tarawa to recuperate and prepare for their next assignment. During that recuperation time, Captain Caldwell asked the members of his company to write a statement about any acts of bravery or heroism they witnessed during Operation Detachment. Caldwell scribbled some notes about several Marines to add to those statements for consideration of military honors. He submitted George for recognition because he had witnessed him carrying a wounded Marine twice his size to safety.

Another person who wrote a statement about George was his Senior Corpsman, Pharmacist Mate First Class, Everett B. Kellogg. He wrote:

On 26 February, 1945, Pharmacist's Mate Second Class Wahlen, although painfully wounded about the left eye [sic]¹, remained on the field of battle and treated a wounded marine who was several yards ahead of the front lines.

He carried this man back to safety while under heavy fire. Wahlen refused to be evacuated, and on 28 February, when an adjacent platoon suffered severe casualties, he went through heavy fire and assisted in the treatment of fourteen men before he returned. On 2 March, Wahlen was again wounded and refused to be evacuated. He moved out with is [sic] platoon in the attack the next day and repeatedly exposed himself to enemy fire to treat wounded Marines on a day when his company received its heaviest casualties in the operation. In the afternoon he was wounded in the foot and unable to walk, Wahlen crawled fifty yards to render first aid to a fallen comrade. He was evacuated late that afternoon. I witnessed these heroic acts and I knew that Wahlen's actions were a constant source of inspiration to the entire company.

A second letter was submitted on George's behalf by Private First Class Glenn D. Chanslor, of the 1st Platoon. He wrote:

On 26 February, 1945 while I was attached to a Marine rifle platoon, I saw Pharmacist's Mate Wahlen proceed approximately twenty five yards to the front of our company lines to administer first aid to a seriously wounded Marine. While

enroute and while rendering first aid he was constantly under fire of mortars, grenades and enemy small arms fire. Though he himself was painfully wounded, prior to undertaking this courageous deed he stayed with the wounded Marine until it was possible to evacuate him to safety. Wahlen refused evacuation for his own wounds, and remained with the company through some of its most difficult fighting.

When asked about George, Chanslor freely admitted, "He was a hero. There was no question about it. I mean when anybody yelled, he was there… boom… no hesitation whatsoever. The guy, it was though he just didn't care whether he lived or died, he did his duty."

*Glenn D. Chanslor of
Wilmar, California*

Both letters were sent up the chain of command with the recommendation from Captain Caldwell.

On April 27, 1945, Colonel Amedeo Rea, who replaced Colonel Joseph P. Sayers, also submitted an endorsement of George's nomination for the Medal of Honor. His suggested citation read:

> *"Pharmacist's Mate Wahlen displayed extraordinary heroism in action from 19 February until evacuated from his unit 3 March 1945. On 26 February, though painfully wounded in the left eye [sic]* [2]*, he remained on the battlefield, administering first aid to a marine who was wounded in front of the company lines. After administering first aid he carried the Marine back to safety through heavy enemy fire. Again on 28 February, when the adjacent platoon suffered severe casualties, Wahlen voluntarily went through heavy mortar and rifle fire to give assistance. Working under constant enemy fire, he treated a total of fourteen men before returning to his platoon. On 2 March Wahlen, again wounded, refused to leave the field, and moved out with the company in attack the next day. During the attack, with utter disregard for his own safety, he repeatedly treated wounded men while exposed to heavy fire. In the afternoon, unable to walk due to a third wound, he crawled forward fifty yards to render first aid to a fallen comrade. Wahlen's actions were inspirational to the men, and influential in the company's success."* [3]

This endorsement was sent to the Secretary of the Navy, via Colonel Chester B. Graham, the commander of the 26th Marines. The next day, 28 April 1945, Colonel Graham endorsed the recommendation, and sent it up to General Keller E. Rockey for his endorsement. On 2 May 1945, General Rockey sent his second endorsement to the Navy Department Board of Decorations and Medals.

At this point, the paper trail becomes much harder to follow, and as a result, the Navy's system of communication breaks down with the Marine Corps. In early September at the Naval Hospital at Santa Margarita Ranch, George was awarded two Navy Crosses (one Navy Cross, and a Gold Star in lieu of a second Navy Cross), signed by General Holland M. Smith of the Marines. From 2 May through September, a third endorsement from the Navy Department Board of Decorations and Medals erroneously recommended that George be "posthumously awarded the Medal of Honor, in lieu of Navy Cross, and Gold Star in lieu of Second Navy Cross."

On 13 September, Fleet Admiral Ernest J. King approved a fourth endorsement of George's recommendation, but repeated the erroneous assumption that "the Medal of Honor be posthumously awarded," in lieu of the Navy Cross and Gold Star "previously approved by the Commanding General, Fleet Marine Force, Pacific," or General H. M. Smith. This endorsement was approved on 14 September by A. L. Gates, acting Secretary of the Navy.

On 22 September, 1945, H. G. Patrick, a retired Navy captain serving in Medals and Awards, sent a memorandum to the Secretary of the Navy stating:

"There is forwarded herewith the citation for the award of the Medal of Honor to George E. Wahlen, Pharmacist's Mate second class, U.S. Naval Reserve, for the signature of the president.

Wahlen is scheduled to be a recipient at the presentation of the Medal of Honor awards on 5 October, 1945."

H. G. Patrick

The suggested citation reads:

"For gallantry and intrepidity at the risk of his life above and beyond the call of duty and without detriment to the mission of his command in the line of his profession in action against the enemy on IWO JIMA, VOLCANO ISLANDS, while attached to a Marine rifle company during the period of 19 February to 3 March, 1945. On 26 February, though painfully wounded in the left eye [sic] [4], Pharmacist's Mate WAHLEN remained on the battlefield, and went forward to render first aid to a Marine who was wounded in front of the company's lines, carrying him back to safety though heavy fire. WAHLEN then remained on duty with the company through its periods of heaviest fighting, constantly disregarding his own safety in order to render first aid to wounded Marines. On 28 February, when the adjacent platoon suffered severe casualties, WAHLEN voluntarily went through heavy mortar and rifle fire to give assistance, and worked under continuous fire, treating a total of fourteen men before returning to his platoon. On 2 March, WAHLEN, again painfully wounded in the back, refused to leave the field, and moved out with the company in attack the next day. During the attack, which was over six hundred yards of open terrain, WAHLEN, with utter disregard for his own safety, repeatedly

treated wounded men while exposed to fire on a day when the company received its heaviest casualties of the operation. In the afternoon, unable to walk due to a third wound received, he crawled forward fifty yards to render first aid to a fallen comrade. His performance of duty rendered him heroic in the minds of his comrades, and the knowledge that WAHLEN would perform his duty of treating wounded under any circumstances inspired confidence in the company, and was influential in its success. His conduct was in keeping with the highest traditions of the United States Naval Service." [5]

This version of the citation was apparently unacceptable, for it was again changed to its final version.

On October 1, 1945, the Navy Department issued a press and radio release, announcing "President to Present Medal of Honor to George E. Wahlen." It went on to say that "George Edward Wahlen, Pharmacist's Mate Second Class, U.S.N.R. of Ogden, Utah will receive the Medal of Honor from President Harry S. Truman on October 5 in recognition of his heroism and self-sacrifice in caring for Marines wounded at Iwo Jima. The award will be presented at the White House in a ceremony held in connection with Nimitz Day." The citation, in its final version read:

Citation:

"For conspicuous gallantry and intrepidity at the risk of his life above and beyond the call of duty while serving with the 2nd Battalion, 26th Marines, 5th Marine Division, during action against enemy Japanese forces on Iwo Jima in the Volcano group on 3 March 1945.

Painfully wounded in the bitter action on 26 February, Wahlen remained on the battlefield, advancing well forward of the frontlines to aid a wounded marine and carrying him back to safety despite a terrific concentration of fire. Tireless in his ministrations, he consistently disregarded all danger to attend his fighting comrades as they fell under the devastating rain of shrapnel and bullets, and rendered prompt assistance to various elements of his combat group as required. When an adjacent platoon suffered heavy casualties, he defied the continuous pounding of heavy mortars and deadly fire of enemy rifles to care for the wounded, working rapidly in an area swept by constant fire and treating 14 casualties before returning to his own platoon. Wounded again on 2 March, he gallantly refused evacuation, moving out with his company the following day in a furious assault across 600 yards of open terrain and repeatedly rendering medical aid while exposed to the blasting fury of powerful Japanese guns. Stouthearted and indomitable, he persevered in his determined efforts as his unit waged fierce battle and, unable to walk after sustaining a third agonizing wound, resolutely crawled 50 yards to administer first aid to still another fallen fighter. By his dauntless fortitude and valor, Wahlen served as a constant inspiration and contributed vitally to the high morale of his company during critical phases of this strategically important engagement. His heroic spirit of self-sacrifice in the face of overwhelming enemy fire upheld the highest traditions of the U.S. Naval Service."

Some publications have erroneously written that George was decorated with both the Medal of Honor and two Navy crosses (Navy Cross with a Gold Star). Because the Navy erroneously assumed that George received the Medal of Honor posthumously, evidence appears to have been lost that he actually received the Navy Crosses. The Navy has never, to George's knowledge, requested that he return the Navy Cross and Gold Star. The language from the Navy assumed that George was deceased, and that he would receive the Medal of Honor in lieu of the Navy Crosses. However, no documentation can be found indicating that the Marine Corps intended to recall the Navy Cross and Gold Star.

For the record, George does not purport to be decorated with both the Medal of Honor, and the two Navy Crosses, although both medals are in his possession.

APPENDIX B

TIMELINE

8 August 1924	George Edward Wahlen (GEW) born
24 October 1929	Wall Street crashes, plunging the world into the "Great Depression"
7 December 1941	Imperial Japanese Forces bomb Pearl Harbor, initiating U.S. entry in to WWII
8 December 1941	GEW enters aircraft engine mechanic's course at Utah Agricultural College in Logan, Utah
11 June 1943	GEW officially inducted in the United States Navy
19 June 1943	GEW reports for basic training, Naval Training Center in San Diego
6 January 1944	GEW reports for duty at Camp Elliot, assigned to Marine Corp
6 June 1944	D-day for "Operation Overlord," the Allied invasion of Normandy
22 July 1944	GEW and the 26th Marines sail from port of San Diego, ultimately destined for Camp Tarawa in Hawaii.
4 January 1945	GEW and the 26th Marines leave port of Hilo, Hawaii
5 February 1945	GEW and invasion convoy reaches Eniwetok
11 February 1945	GEW and invasion convoy reaches Saipan, final stop before Iwo Jima

19 February 1945	D-day on Iwo Jima; GEW lands with the 26th Marines
3 March 1945	GEW evacuated from Iwo Jima
7 May 1945	Nazi Germany surrenders
6 August 1945	Atomic bomb dropped on Hiroshima
14 August 1945	President Truman announces Japanese surrender
2 September 1945	Japan signs "unconditional surrender" on USS *Missouri*
14 September 1945	GEW receives Navy Cross, and Gold Star in lieu of second Navy Cross
5 October 1945	GEW receives Medal of Honor from President Harry S. Truman
19 December 1945	GEW discharged from military duty
16 August 1946	GEW marries Melba Holley of Slaterville, Utah
13 August 1948	GEW graduates Weber College
28 November 1948	GEW enlists in the U.S. Army
15 July 1959	GEW commissioned a first lieutenant
11 August 1969	GEW retires from military service
6 December 2003	President George W. Bush signs legislation authorizing VA medical facility in Salt Lake City to be named the "George E. Wahlen Department of Veterans Affairs Medical Center"
10 November 2004	"George E. Wahlen Department of Veterans Affairs Medical Center" dedicated.

In Memoriam

This book is devoted to the memory of all the young men who died on Iwo Jima, but especially the 67 men of "F" Company, 2nd Battalion, 26th Regiment of the 5th Marine Division whose sacrifice we must never forget. May their souls rest in peace.

Pfc. Gaitano Arcuri
Pfc. Charles B. Bachelor
Pfc. John I. Beck
Pfc. Frank E. Becker
Pfc. Joseph E. Bizyozez
2nd Lt. James W. Cassidy
Pvt. Frank O. Cauffman
2nd Lt. Earnest A. Clark
Pvt. James C. Collar
Cpl. Francis P. Corrigan
Asst. Ck. George J. Dancin
Sgt. John W. Danielson
Sgt. Robert W. Dickenson
Pfc. William D. Donegan
Pltn. Sgt. Burchard J. Drake
Pfc. Joe C. Farinella
Pvt. Armando H. Felix
Pfc. Verdin W. Fitch
Cpl. John C. Folsom
Pfc. John E. Forbes
Pfc. Daniel P. Francis
Cpl. Jewel W. Gaither
Pfc. Ilario Garcia
Pfc. Joseph J. Gazda
2nd Lt. Martin L. Gelshenen
Pfc. Donald C. Gregory
Pvt. Alvin G. Harris
Pfc. Richard H. Heinen
Pfc. Ralph J. Hengel
Cpl. Sidney J. Hill
Pfc. Clinton F. Hinton
1st Sgt. John W. Horner
Cpl. Marion N. Howell
Cpl. William T. Irwin

Pfc. Harley F. Jacobson
Pfc. Robert R. Johnson
Pvt. Walter E. Johnston
Pvt. Charles C. Kraucunas
Pfc. James E. Krussell
Pfc. Melvin F. Kurzawski
Pvt. James H. Lungren
Pfc. John N. Manahan
Pfc. Thomas F. Marisak
Pfc. Andrew M. Martin, Jr.
1st Lt. William D. Martt
Pfc. Irwin L. McKinnon
Pfc. Raymon E. Mercier
Pfc. Charles W. Miller
Pfc. William L. Mintling
Pfc. Francis E. Mitchel
PM3C. Edward Monjaras
Pfc. Joseph F. Moran
Pfc. Charles E. Murray
Pfc. Ray H. Padgett
Pfc. Thomas L. Patterson
Sgt. Robert E. Poarche
Pfc. Alfred F. Riina
Pfc. Conrad F. Sorenson
Pvt. Lawrence D. Staples
Cpl. Harold E. Trentham
Pfc. John J. Vitanyi
Pfc. Richard M. Von Egidy
Pvt. Lawrence J. Walker
Pvt. Russell Ward
Pfc. Louis F. Warenczak
Pfc. Richard M. West
Pfc. William T. White

ACKNOWLEDGMENTS

The completion of this book was a labor of love. Many people who contributed to this work also seem to have felt this way, and it has been evident to me in their work, patience, and diligence as they helped me research, compile, and capture this story. First of all, please permit me to express my sincere thanks to those who have helped bring this project to completion.

In particular, this book would not have come to fruition without the kind and able assistance of a few key men from George's unit: (alphabetically) Frank Caldwell, Bob DeGeus, Dean Keeley, and Rudy Mueller, of Fox Company, 2nd Battalion, 26th Marines, 5th Marine Division.

Rudy Mueller is the institutional memory of Fox Company. He has conducted extensive research throughout the years, and has been eager to provide detailed information to assist my investigation. His wife, Jeanne, likewise has been accessible and helpful in offering timely responses to my incessant questions. Every combat group needs a Rudy Mueller. Almost single-handedly he has preserved the legacy of Fox Company for generations to come. Indeed, I feel fortunate to have come to know him, as I fear to contemplate the lengths I would have gone to obtain the information I received from him.

I have also relished my interactions with Dr. Dean Keeley, who has been willing to share both his insights and some of his most painful experiences. He is a great man, and I appreciate all he has done to assist me, including his willingness to review the manuscript in its final stages. He has suffered greatly throughout his life as a result of his heroic actions on Iwo Jima. His story, too, is amazing, and he deserves a book of his own.

Bob DeGeus has likewise been very helpful in providing additional resources for my research. He is a kind, good-hearted man who has bent over backwards to help me. I am also obligated to him for his willingness to share his artistic talents for this project.

I am truly indebted to Col. Frank Caldwell, who spent countless hours on the telephone with me. Not only did he share his experiences, but he offered me precious details about each day he spent on Iwo Jima. After exhausting all available resources, I relied on him to help me fill in the gaps. He has patiently endured my endless questions with thoughtful, well-spoken responses. I also appreciate his skills as a technical editor, as he reviewed the manuscript to ensure I had my facts straight.

I am fortunate to have been introduced to Richard Overton. He has written what I believe to be the quintessential firsthand account of a corpsman on Iwo Jima. His book *God Isn't Here: A Young American's Entry Into World War II, and His Participation in the Battle for Iwo Jima* was crucial to my research. I would have spent many additional months in research had it not been for his extensive notes and the detailed accounts of his time spent on Iwo Jima. I also appreciate his enthusiasm for this project and for his expert review. It's an honor to have come to know both Dick and Joan Overton. I consider them dear friends.

Without question, the most time-consuming task was conducting my research. Many excellent sources exist which were helpful in giving me the basic knowledge of the battle for Iwo Jima. But the most intriguing sources were the veterans who were there. At some point I interviewed each of the following people, who were kind enough to spend hours in some cases, discussing their experience on Iwo Jima. They are R.A. Aubrey, Glenn D. Chanslor, Thomas J. Farkas, Eugene C. Hansen, Peter N. Karegeannes, Sr., Everett B. Kellogg, Edward F. McHenry, Edward E. Muich, Robert L. Ray, John Repko, and Jack Russell. I thank them for their time and kindness.

As the writing process concluded, I am grateful to my editors Tanna Berry and Chris Rosenquist for their editing skills and their patience with me as they guided me through the editing process. Tanna was the first editor on this project. She helped me sharpen the focus of the book and expand the topics that required further explanation. She has a unique skill for seeing the big picture, while articulating the details necessary to help me write the best story of which I am capable.

Chris Rosenquist has been an invaluable resource. She was especially skilled at helping me tighten the story line and refine the text. As with all good editors, she has the ability to identify the gaps in the story and help me explain what needed to be said. I am grateful for the extensive experience that she brings to this project, having previously edited other WWII projects. Her dedication was a reflection of her gratitude to all veterans; but specifically she became involved in this project to honor her uncle, PFC Dean Perkins, Battery D, 2nd Battalion, 13th Regiment, 5th Marine Division, who served on Iwo Jima. It has been an honor working with her.

Don Norton must also be recognized for his contribution in editing the final text. He caught several significant errors, and was instrumental in ensuring that the galley copy was ready for print. His quick turnaround helped us to meet our final deadline. I also appreciate the keen eye of Shannon Solomon, who served as a proofreader.

My friend and colleague, Margie Esquibel, has the uncanny ability to see errors that others may have missed. She was kind enough to have the final edit. I thank her for making the tremendous effort to help. Despite her dislike for proofreading, she has has a keen eye for details.

I appreciate the willingness of those who offered their endorsements, specifically Harlan Glenn, James Bradley, and Doug Sterner. Your kind words of encouragement are most cherished.

It is an honor to have the names of Senators Bob Dole and Orrin Hatch on this book.

Senator Dole is a great American, whose service to this country is unmatched when it comes to advocating the needs of veterans. I can think of no better person to represent the quiet heroes of the "Greatest Generation." I also appreciate the efforts of Mike Marshall from Senator Dole's office, who was kind enough to follow through with all the details.

I am equally honored to have Senator Orrin Hatch contribute the introduction. Senator Hatch has worked closely with George on several projects, and has always been willing to lend his support to veterans' causes. I am grateful for Senator Hatch's kind words and ongoing support. I would also be remiss if I didn't mention Melanie Bowen and Heather Barney from Senator Hatch's office. Both went the extra mile to assist me in this project, and their efforts are greatly appreciated.

I owe a major debt of gratitude to my family, who endured my absence during this entire project. Although I have physically been available, I have spent almost every free minute at the computer. When I asked their permission to pursue this project, I warned them of the time commitment necessary to write and produce this book; however, I appreciate their patience, since I don't think they fully realized just how much this project would consume my life. Their complaints have been minimal, and their patience has been considerable. Thank you and I love you.

It has been an incredible honor getting to know George and Melba Wahlen. They have gone to great lengths to oblige my prying questions. I have dug deep into their past, and they have been accommodating at every step. George has been exceptionally forthcoming as he has opened up his life and shared with me his innermost thoughts. Without exception, he has responded candidly to every inquiry I have thrown at him. Some memories are painful, yet he dutifully explained the circumstances and details of each agonizing event. As I have watched George in many public settings as he poses for pictures, signs autographs, and shakes hands with well-wishers, he remains the most humble man I know. He truly dislikes being the focus of the attention, but he endures it well. I am grateful for both George and Melba's kindness, and I am honored to call them friends.

Above all, I thank God for guiding me throughout this project. I have grown in many ways as I have struggled to complete it. I recognize His hand in every aspect of this book, as I have witnessed His guidance and inspiration at every turn. I continue to be blessed beyond measure.

Helpful Terms

George E. Wahlen was assigned to 1st Platoon, "F" or Fox Company, 2nd Battalion, 26th Marine Regiment, 5th Marine Division, Fleet Marine Force. For the purpose of this book, the company, battalion, and regiments will be abbreviated by their battalion and regiment; thus George was F/2/26. Often, the company will not be identified, just the battalion and regiment; thus 2/26 refers to the 2nd Battalion, 26th Marine Regiment.

Amtrac - "amphibious tractor" or "amphibious vehicle for troops" A flat-bottomed motor vehicle that can move on land or water, used to transport troops from ship to shore in preparation for an attack.

APA - Amphibious/Attack Transports were designed to sail to the site of amphibious operations carrying assault troops and support equipment. APA/LPAs had the capacity to hold a full battalion of troops. The APA disembarked troops with the ships own landing craft. The APA would then stand off the beachhead ready to evacuate troops, casualties, and prisoners of war. In order to carry out its primary mission, APAs had to provide all facilities for the embarked troops, including berthing, messing , medical and dental care, and recreational facilities. All APAs in the Navy inventory on 1 January 1969 were redesignated LPAs.

B-29 bomber - The Boeing B-29 Superfortress was an American four-engine heavy bomber and one of the largest aircraft of WWII to see active service. It was the primary U.S. strike weapon against Japan and continued to serve long after the war was over.

BAR man - Rifleman carrying a Browning Automatic Rifle.

Betty - Japanese patrol bomber or torpedo plane.

Boatswain - (Also bo'sun) A petty officer whose main duties pertain to deck and boat seamanship. Pronounced BO-son.

Boondockers – Marine boots or shoes.

Brig - Prison on a ship or shore base.

Convoy - An assembly of ships organized in columns and escorted by warships.

Chancre - Term for lesions caused by sexually transmitted disease. Also shin bruises caused by collision with ladders and combings. A common ailment.

Buck Sergeant - Three-stripe sergeant.

Bulkhead - Wall aboard ship.

CO - Commanding Officer

Company - A subdivision of a military regiment or battalion that constitutes the lowest administrative unit. It is usually under the command of a captain and is made up of at least two platoons.

Corpsman - An enlisted person in the U.S. Navy or Marines who has been trained to give first aid and basic medical treatment, especially in combat situations.

Corsair - Without a doubt, the Navy's strongest fighter, with its distinctive inverted gull wing, the Chance Vought F4U. Designed as a powerful carrier fighter, the early F4Us were restricted to land bases because they were difficult to fly aboard ship. But by the end of 1944 Navy and Marine squadrons were safely operating aboard carriers.

D-day – Debarkation day. Commonly associated with the June 1944 Allied landing at Normandy, France.

DUKW - An amphibious vehicle, also known as a Duck, used to transport troops from a ship to the beach.

Eniwetok - (or Enewetak) an atoll in the Marshall Isands of the central Pacific Ocean. Its land consists of about 40 small islets totaling less than 6 sq km, surrounding a lagoon, 80 km (50 mi) in circumference. Enewetak was captured by Japan in 1914 and mandated to them by the League of Nations in 1920. The Japanese mostly ignored the atoll until WWII. In November 1942, they built an airfield on Engebi Island, which was used for staging planes to the Carolines and the rest of the Marshalls. When the Gilberts fell to the U.S., the Japanese army's 1st Amphibious Brigade came in to defend the atoll, January 4, 1944 . They were unable to finish fortifying the place before the February launch of Operation Catchpole, which captured all the islets in a week.

Foxhole - Same as rifle pit, a hole dug for protection, and from which to fight.

F.M.F. - Fleet Marine Force

Gunny - Gunnery Sergeant

H hour – The hour at which an operation begins.

Hellcats - The Hellcat was the main shipboard fighter of the U.S. Navy for the last two years of the Pacific War. The F6F was ordered for the U.S. Navy after the initial shock of Allied contact with superior Japanese fighters, particularly the Mitsubishi A6M Zero, during the first few months of the Pacific War. As a result of this experience of combat against higher-performance machines, the Hellcat's specification required the most powerful engine available.

Higgins boat - Generic name for the flat-bottomed landing craft created specially for Overlord by Andrew Higgins; each type had a different codename (see L).

KaBar - (KAY-bar) a solid fixed blade knife short enough to be swung quickly, yet long enough to cause significant internal damage to an enemy combatant.

LCI - Landing Craft, Infantry

LCT - Landing Craft, Tank

LCVP - Landing Craft, Vehicles and Personnel

Leatherneck - A United States Marine, from the high leather collar formerly worn with formal uniforms.

LSM - Landing Ship, Medium

LST - Landing Ship, Tank

M-1 - Garand rifle

MP- Military Police

Mess Deck - Location of the crew's eating area.

Muster - To assemble the crew; roll call.

Marine units and their approximate size during WWII.

> Marine <u>Division</u> – A division accounts for over 20,000 men. (The 5th Marine division contained the 26th, 27th, 28th and 13th Marine Regiments, as well as an Engineer, Pioneer, Tank, Service, Motor Transport, Medical, and two Amphibian Tractor Battalions, a Signal and Laundry Company, a War Dog platoon, an observation squadron, and two replacement battalions.)

> Marine <u>Regiment</u> – A regiment accounts for about 3,300 men. The 26th Marine Regiment, designated at 2/26, or the 26th Marines for short. A regiment was comprised of three battalions.

> Marine <u>Battalion</u> – A battalion accounts for about 1,100 men. A battalion was comprised of three companies.

> Marine <u>Company</u> – Comprised of about 250 men (including Marines, corpsman and officers). In the case of George Wahlen, he was assigned to "F" or Fox Company, but "D" or Dog Company and "E" or Easy Company were also part of the 26th Marine regiment.

> <u>Platoon</u> – A typical rifle platoon consisted of approximately 45 men; 43 Marines, 2 Navy corpsmen (mortar platoons were smaller, with about 18-20 men; Machine Gun platoons had as many at 56 men).

M4A3 tank - The M4 General Sherman tank was the main tank designed and built by the U.S. for use in World War II. It was named after Union General William Tecumseh Sherman. The name is often shortened to M4 Sherman or simply Sherman. Its high profile and rounded top made it an easy target, but it was rather fast and maneuverable, reliable, and easy to produce and service.

NCO - A non-commissioned officer is an enlisted soldier or sailor who has been delegated leadership or command authority by a commissioned officer.

PFC- Private First Class

P-51 Mustang - The North American P-51 Mustang was a successful long-range fighter aircraft which set new standards of excellence and performance when it entered service in the middle years of World War II and is still regarded as one of the very best piston-engined fighters ever made.

R & R- Rest and Relaxation

Saipan - Part of the Marianas Islands in the Pacific. U.S. troops made an amphibious assault on the Japanese-held island on June 15,1944. The Japanese troops surrendered on July 7, 1944.

Shelter half - Also known as a "dog tent" or "pup tent," is a simple kind of tent. Two sheets of canvas or a similar material (the halves) are fastened together with snaps or straps to form a larger surface. The shelter half is then erected using poles, ropes, pegs, and whatever tools are on hand, forming an inverted V structure.

Squadron - 1) An organization consisting of two or more divisions of ships, or two or more divisions (Navy) or flights of aircraft. It is normally, but not necessarily composed of ships or aircraft of the same type; 2) the basic administrative aviation unit of the Army, Navy, Marine Corps, and Air Force; 3) battalion-size ground or aviation units in U.S. Army cavalry regiments.

Strafing - (adaptation of German strafen - to punish) is the practice of shooting a machine gun, from an airplane in-flight, at objects or people on the ground.

USO - The United Service Organizations (USO) was established to provide support to U.S. military personnel around the world. The USO is made up entirely of volunteers. Its goal is to make life easier for U.S. soldiers. Its most publicized focus is "USO tours," which include top billed celebrities.

Wardroom - Officers assembly and mess room aboard a Navy ship.

NOTES AND SOURCES

Chapter 4 - Training to Training
 [1] *History of the Marines*, Howe,Ludwig,Shaw, p. 51
 [2] *home.att.net/~corpsman/field_equipment_of_a_wwii_corpsm.htm*
 David Steinert, and George B. Lusk, CMC, Naval Hospital Camp Pendleton
 [3] *www.cpp.usmc.mil/cpao/pages/about/history/preparing_marines.htm* , USMC,
 Camp Pendleton
 [4] *The Spearhead*, Conner, p. 1
 [5] Interview, Frank Caldwell
 [6] Interview, Peter Karegeannes
 [7] Interview, Frank Caldwell
 [8] Interview, Dean Keeley
 [9] *God Isn't Here*, Overton, p. 87

Chapter 5 - Hawaii is Hell
 [1] *God Isn't Here*, Overton, p. 89
 [2] *The Spearhead*, Conner, p. 15
 [3] *www.bestplaceshawaii.com/island_insights/bigisland/floraFauna.html*
 Best Places Hawaii, H&S Publishing, LLC,
 [4] Ibid
 [5] Interview, Dean Keeley
 [6] *www.ibiblio.org/hyperwar/USMC/USMC-M-IwoJima/USMC-M-IwoJima-2.html#cn48*
 Historical Section, USMC
 [7] *www.csd.uwo.ca/%7Epettypi/elevon/baugher_us/b029-10.html* University of
 Western Ontario
 [8] 2/26 After Action Report (AAR), Sayers, p. 1

Chapter 6 - Finding God
 [1] Interview, Frank Caldwell
 [2] *God Isn't Here*, Overton, p. 133
 [3] *The Spearhead*, Conner, p. 29
 [4] Ibid
 [5] Ibid
 [6] Ibid, p. 30

Chapter 7 - "Operation Detachment"
[1] *www.ibiblio.org/hyperwar/USMC/IV/USMC-IV-VI-3.html* , Historical Section, USMC
[2] *americanhistory.about.com/library/prm/blwarinletters.htm*, About, Inc. A PRIMEDIA Company.
[3] *Closing In: Marines in the Seizure of Iwo Jima*, Alexander, p. 9
[4] *www.ibiblio.org/hyperwar/USMC/IV/USMC-IV-VI-3.html* , Historical Section, USMC

Chapter 8 - D-day, February 19, 1945
[1] *God Isn't Here*, Overton, p. 124
[2] *The Spearhead*, Conner, p. 43
[3] Interview, Frank C. Caldwell
[4] *The Spearhead*, Conner, p. 44
[5] *God Isn't Here*, Overton, p. 124
[6] *The Spearhead*, Conner, p. 47
[7] *Closing In: Marines in the Seizure of Iwo Jima*, Alexander, p. 17
[8] *Iwo Jima*, Newcomb, p. 100
[9] *Closing In: Marines in the Seizure of Iwo Jima*, Alexander, p. 17
[10] *The Spearhead*, Conner, p. 47
[11] *Closing In: Marines in the Seizure of Iwo Jima*, Alexander, p. 14
[12] The troops aboard the USS *Hocking* were CT-2-26 (CT=Combat Team) or 2nd Battalion, 26th Regiment
[13] Interview, Jack Russell
[14] *The Spearhead*, Conner, p. 49
[15] 2/26 AAR, p. 5
[16] Interview, Rudy Mueller
[17] Interview, Thomas J. Farkas

Chapter 9 - D-day Afternoon
[1] *The Spearhead*, Conner, p. 49 ; *www.geocities.com/mnjhession/honor_your_father.htm*, By Matthew Hession and Joan Hession
[2] Ibid
[3] *God Isn't Here*, Overton p. 170
[4] Interview, Frank Caldwell

Chapter 10 D+1 and D+2 - The First Casualty
[1] *The Spearhead*, Conner, p. 74
[2] *Closing In: Marines in the Seizure of Iwo Jima*, Alexander p. 14
[3] Ibid, p. 24
[4] 2/26 AAR, p. 6

[5] Spearhead, Conner, p. 74
[6] 2/26 AAR, p. 6
[7] Ibid, p. 5
[8] Interview, Robert L. Ray,
[9] Interview, Thomas L. Farkas
[10] 2/26 AAR, p. 5

Chapter 11 - D+3: This Lousy, Stinking Island
[1] 2-26 AAR, p. 6
[2] 2-26 AAR p. 6 Reports moving to 181 H,J, coordinates on V Corp operations map.
[3] Interview, Dean Keeley
[4] 2-26, AAR, p. 6
[5] Ibid
[6] Interview, Frank Caldwell
[7] 2-26 AAR, p. 6

Chapter 12 - D+4: A Shift in Momentum
[1] 2-26 AAR, p. 7
[2] Interview, Everett Kellogg
[3] *www.eyewitnesstohistory.com/iwoflag.htm*
[4] Marines in the Seizure of Iwo Jima, Alexander, p. 27
[5] Because of the power of the Joe Rosenthal image, well-wishers wanted to identify the faceless men in the photo. After weeks of searching, the names of the Marine flag raisers were identified as Sergeant Michael Strank, Pharmacists Mate Second Class John H. Bradley; Corporal Harlan H. Block; and Privates Ira H. Hayes, Franklin R. Sousely and Rene A. Gagnon. They became instant celebrities that were called upon in subsequent months and years to talk about their experience raising the flag. The fact that these men were the second flag raisers wasn't widely known for some time.
[6] Closing In: Marines Seizure of Iwo Jima, Alexander, p. 27
[7] *God Isn't Here*, Overton, p. 173

Chapter 13 - D+5 and D+6: The Calm Before The Storm
[1] 2-26 AAR, p. 7
[2] Interview, Frank Caldwell

Chapter 14 - D+7 a.m.: The Crucible
[1] Dispatch Summary, 5th MarDiv 26 Feb 1945
[2] Mueller, *Fox Company Scoop*, May 2004, p. 14
[3] 2-26 AAR, p. 7

[4] Ibid.
[5] Interview, Frank Caldwell
[6] Interview, Jack Russell
[7] Ibid.

Chapter 15 - D+7: It's My Job...No More...No Less
[1] 2-26 AAR, p. 8
[2] *The Spearhead*, Conner, p. 85
[3] 2-26 AAR, p. 7
[4] Ibid.
[5] *Iwo Jima*, Newcomb, p. 197
[6] 2-26 AAR, p. 8
[7] *Our War Years*, Fox Company, Mueller, pp. 53-54

Chapter 16 - D+8: Regimental Reserve
[1] *www.usarmymodels.com/ARTICLES/Rations/10in1rations.html*, Modeling the U.S. Army in WWII. Timothy S. Streeter
[2] 2-26 AAR, p. 7
[3] Jan Herman, Interview with George Wahlen, 1996 p. 15
[4] Since Iwo Jima, George has continued to suffer from grenade fragments still lodged in his face and backside. On occasion these metal pieces have worked their way to his skin's surface.

Chapter 17 - D+9: Dig and Hold
[1] 2-26 AAR, p. 8
[2] Interview, Frank Caldwell
[3] *The Spearhead*, Conner, p. 90. (Willis was posthumously awarded the Medal of Honor. He joined George Wahlen as the second corpsman from the 5th Marine Division to earn that honor.)
[4] Ibid, p. 90
[5] *Iwo Jima*, Newcomb, p. 199
[6] Ibid, p. 207
[7] 2-26 AAR, p. 9

Chapter 18 - D+10: Taking Hill 362A
[1] Interview, Frank Caldwell
[2] Dispatch Summary, 5th MarDiv, Mar 1, 1945
[3] *Iwo Jima*, Newcomb, pp. 208-9
[4] 2-26 AAR, p. 9
[5] *God Isn't Here*, Overton, p. 143

[6] Our War Years, Fox Company, Mueller, pp. 53-54
[7] Dispatch Summary, 5th MarDiv, Mar 1, 1945,

Chapter 19 - D+11: Caught From Behind
  [1] *The Spearhead*, Conner, p. 93
  [2] Dispatch Summary, 5th MarDiv, Mar 2, 1945
  [3] 2-26 AAR , p. 10
  [4] Dispatch Summary, 5th MarDiv, Mar 2, 1945
  [5] Ibid
  [6] Dispatch Summary, 5th MarDiv, 1 Mar 1945
  [7] 2-26 AAR, p. 10

Chapter 20 - D+12: The Final Act of Heroism
  [1] Dispatch Summary, 5th MarDiv, Mar 3, 1945
  [2] Interview, Frank Caldwell
  [3] Ibid
  [4] 2-26 AAR, p. 11
  [5] *Our War Years*, Fox Company, Mueller, pp. 53-54

Chapter 22 - From Patient to "Pill Pusher"
  [1] *San Diego Blade-Tribune Progress Edition*, 10/25/1943, p. 78
  [2] Ibid, p. 79
  [3] The nightmares continued until the day he was married. Since that time, he has rarely been bothered with them.
  [4] *www.floridamemory.com/FloridaHighlights/V-J_Day/*, Florida State Archives, Florida Department of State.
  [5] This citation mistakenly indicates the left eye was injured, when in fact, it was the right eye.

Chapter 23 - Home and Discharge
  [1] *Ogden Standard-Examiner*, October 7, 1945, p. 9

Appendix A - Two Navy Crosses for a Medal of Honor
  [1,2] This citation mistakenly indicates the left eye was injured, when in fact, it was the right eye.
  [3] Fourth Endorsement to CO, 2ndBn, 26[th]Mar of 27 April, 1945.
  [4] Enclosure "A," Fourth Endorsement, H. G. Patrick
  [5] This citation mistakenly indicates the left eye was injured, when in fact, it was the right eye.

PHOTOGRAPH / IMAGE CREDITS

Page 6: (Portrait in Navy uniform) Courtesy GEW (George E. Wahlen)
Page 18: National Archives-127-GW-312-112422
Page 20: (On tricycle) Courtesy GEW
Page 22: (Twin Brothers) Courtesy GEW
Page 22: (Wilson Lane School) Courtesy GEW
Page 28: *The Spearhead, 5th Marine Division* USMC, Marine Corps Historical Division, courtesy Edward F. McHenry
Page 29: (Graduation from basic training) GEW
Page 35: *The Spearhead, 5th Marine Division* USMC, Marine Corps Historical Division, courtesy Edward F. McHenry
Page 36: Courtesy Frank C. Caldwell
Page 37: *The Spearhead, 5th Marine Division* USMC, Marine Corps Historical Division, courtesy Edward F. McHenry
Page 38: Edward Monjaras, Courtesy John Monjaras
Page 39: Courtesy Robert D. DeGeus
Page 40: *The Spearhead*, 5th Marine Division USMC, Marine Corps Historical Division, courtesy Edward F. McHenry
Page 47: *The Spearhead*, 5th Marine Division USMC, Marine Corps Historical Division, courtesy Edward F. McHenry
Page 49: Courtesy Dean F. Keeley
Page 51: *The Spearhead*, 5th Marine Division USMC, Marine Corps Historical Division, courtesy Edward F. McHenry
Page 52: Courtesy John Monjaras
Page 58: National Archives-127-GW-330-44574
Page 61: Courtesy Richard E. Overton, Copyright 2004, Used by permission
Page 65: National Archives-127-GW-000-152108
Page 69: U.S. Army Photo - *www.ibiblio.org/hyperwar/ USA/USA-P-Strategy/ #page485*
Page 73: National Archives-127-GW-306-109963
Page 75: National Archives-127-GW-350-110130
Page 77: National Archives-127-GW-352-111686
Page 78: National Archives-127-GW-350-111908
Page 79: National Archives-127-GW-000-109875
Page 80: National Archives-127-GW-294-112633
Page 82: National Archives-127-GW-311-110114
Page 83: National Archives-127-GW-312-111120
Page 85: USMC Historical Collection
Page 86: National Archives-127-GW-304-109909
Page 87: National Archives-127-GW-335-110606
Page 88: National Archives-127-GW-335-111243
Page 89: National Archives-127-GW-313-110297
Page 92: National Archives-127-GW-306-111768
Page 93: National Archives-127-GW-306-109965

Page 94: National Archives-127-GW-306-110182
Page 95: National Archives-127-GW-313-109777
Page 96: National Archives-127-GW-306-109920
Page 103: National Archives-127-GW-000-111006
Page 105: National Archives-127-GW-313-109683
Page 111: National Archives-127-GW-319-116773
Page 112: National Archives-127-GW-319-142859
Page 113: National Archives-127-GW-331-11142

Page 115: National Archives-127-GW-330-109619
Page 117: National Archives-127-GW-307-111173
Page 118: National Archives-127-GW-313-112359
Page 120: National Archives-127-GW-304-119014
Page 124: National Archives-127-GW-343-109702
Page 125: National Archives-127-GW-306-114384
Page 126: National Archives-127-GW-347-114386
Page 127: National Archives-127-GW-306-114385
Page 128: National Archives-127-GW-347-114387
Page 134: National Archives-127-GW-306-110639
Page 135: National Archives-127-GW-313-112253
Page 139: Courtesy Robert D. DeGeus, Copyright 2004. Used by permission
Page 143: National Archives-127-GW-321-111900
Page 144: National Archives-127-GW-329-112802
Page 145: National Archives-127-GW-338-144512
Page 147: National Archives-127-GW-306-112200
Page 152: National Archives-127-GW-318-148982
Page 154: National Archives-127-GW-306-142704
Page 159: National Archives-127-GW-312-112258
Page 161: National Archives-127-GW-306-113278
Page 160: National Archives-127-GW-306-112805
Page 162: National Archives-127-GW-306-112134
Page 168: National Archives-127-GW-306-112855
Page 169: National Archives-127-GW-306-112000
Page 170: National Archives-127-GW-312-111883
Page 171: National Archives-127-GW-331-144032
Page 173: National Archives-127-GW-331-110320
Page 174: National Archives-127-GW-312-111074
Page 177: National Archives-127-GW-331-112315
Page 181: USMC Historical Collection
Page 187: USMC Historical Collection
Page 188: Courtesy GEW
Page 192: Courtesy Everett B. Kellogg
Page 196: Courtesy GEW
Page 198: Courtesy GEW
Page 201: Courtesy GEW
Page 203: Courtesy GEW
Page 204: Courtesy Gary Toyn
Page 209: Courtesy Glenn D. Chanslor

INDEX

In this index the letter *i* is used to indicate an illustration, a *m* is used for maps and a *p* for photo. Ships can be found by *Name*, followed by the designation USS.